WINNING
PULITZERS

WINNING
PULITZERS

The Stories Behind
Some of the Best News Coverage of Our Time

KAREN ROTHMYER

New York ❑ COLUMBIA UNIVERSITY PRESS

Columbia University Press
New York   Oxford

Casebound editions of Columbia University Press books are Smyth-sewn and printed
on permanent and durable acid-free paper

Printed in the United States of America

c 10 9 8 7 6 5 4 3 2 1
p 10 9 8 7 6 5 4 3 2 1

Library of Congress Cataloging-in-Publication Data

Winning Pulitzers : the stories behind some of the best news
   coverage of our time / Karen Rothmyer.
      p.   cm.
   ISBN 0-231-07028-4
   1. Journalists—United States—Interviews.   2. Pulitzer prizes.
   3. Reportage literature, American.   4. Feature stories.
   I. Rothmyer, Karen.
   PN4871.W7   1990
   070'.92'2—dc20   90-49406
                                                                               CIP

CONTENTS

PREFACE

When journalists gather after work to talk about their day, the stories that they tell are not those that will be in tomorrow's newspaper, but rather the stories-behind-the-stories: the hunch that paid off, the search for a document that could be the key to a successful investigation, the encounters with the famous—or infamous—in the course of the day's assignments.

This book is a series of just such stories-behind-the-stories, as recounted to me in a year-long series of interviews with newsmen and newswomen living all over the country. What makes them special is that each involves an example of journalism that won a Pulitzer Prize. These first-person reminiscences provide a ringside seat at some of the major historical events of the twentieth century, from Hiroshima to Vietnam to Iran-contra. In addition, they offer considerable insight into how journalism has been practiced in this country during the first seventy-five years of the Pulitzer Prizes' existence.

Accompanying the stories-behind-the stories are brief excerpts from the prizewinners' entries. These are intended to give a flavor of each writer's work rather than a full sampling of the sort found in a variety of Pulitzer anthologies. Newspaper journalism is, by its nature, ephemeral: much of what it concerns itself with on any given day is unfamiliar or even unknown to succeeding generations of readers. What remains fresh and fascinating ten or even fifty years later are the memories and insights of the people who were there, witnessing social or political history with their own eyes.

In this book, the winning journalists speak for themselves through taped and edited interviews. I asked them to talk not only about their prizewinning entries but also about themselves: what journalism and the world were like as they found them; what conclusions they've reached after years in the news business. Each chapter is devoted to a different winner, and each includes a short introduction, an excerpt from that person's work, and a first-person account.

The decision about which winners to approach was guided by a wish to include as diverse a group as possible in terms of age, type of journalism, and similar considerations. In some cases, the winners were members of teams that won for their collective efforts. In order to give some representation to the early era of the Pulitzer Prizes, I have included several winners who either left behind written recollections or whose prizewinning efforts were the subject of articles by others. In addition to writers, the group includes a news photographer and an editorial cartoonist. It also includes a Pulitzer Prize judge who, although he speaks here only in that capacity, was himself part of a Pulitzer Prize-winning effort.

While I attempted to be as careful as possible in retaining the style and personal voice of each of the winners interviewed, the chapters are condensed and ordered versions of what were sometimes quite long, thoughtful, and pleasantly rambling conversations.

ACKNOWLEDGMENTS

I am grateful to all the Pulitzer Prize winners and judges who took the time to talk with me about their experiences.

Thanks go to Pulitzer Prize Board administrator Robert Christopher, who offered encouragement for the project, and to his associate Edward (Bud) Kliment, for his assistance in numerous matters including helping to locate prizewinners.

I am indebted to retired Pulitzer Prize Board administrator John Hohenberg, whose books *The Pulitzer Prizes, The Pulitzer Prize Story*, and *The Pulitzer Prize Story II*, provided an invaluable account of the early history of the prizes as well as considerable information about the prizes and prizewinners through the years. Dr. Csillag Andras shared with me the insights into Joseph Pulitzer he had gathered in the course of research in Hungary and in the United States.

My thanks go to my editor at Columbia University Press, Jennifer Crewe, and to my students, colleagues, and family for their support.

Grateful acknowledgment is made to the following for permission to reprint material: the *New York Times;* the Associated Press; the Louisville *Courier-Journal,* Whitney Communications (successor to the *New York Herald Tribune*); the *Seattle Times;* the Fargo (N.D.) *Forum* (formerly *The Fargo Forum*); the *Detroit Free Press;* the *Miami Herald;* the San Diego *Evening Tribune;* the *Georgia Gazette;* the *Denver Post;* the *Los Angeles Times;* Stanley Forman; Paul Conrad; and Simon & Schuster, Inc.

WINNING
PULITZERS

INTRODUCTION

Former Pulitzer Prize Board member Osborn Elliott recalls a conversation in the early 1980s with columnist Jimmy Breslin, the quintessential street-smart guy who doesn't care a damn about anybody's opinion. At the time, Breslin was already established as one of the most famous journalists on the East Coast and certainly one of only a handful with national reputations. But it wasn't enough. "He called up one day and he'd obviously been visiting the bars in Queens," Elliott recalls with amusement. "He said, 'Why aren't you bastards ever going to give me a Pulitzer Prize?'"

As it happened, Breslin did later win a Pulitzer—not, Elliott hastens to add, because of any phone calls. But what's most revealing about the incident is that it shows just how much the Pulitzer Prizes in journalism mean to the thousands of writers and editors working at America's more than 1600 daily and 7000 or so weekly newspapers. Despite occasional scandals and more than their share of criticism through the years, the prizes, which have been given annually since 1917 for excellence in newspaper journalism, represent the highest professional honor attainable in the life of any American journalist. And it doesn't stop there. As 1959 Pulitzer Prize winner Mary Lou Werner Forbes jokes, "It's going to look great in my obituary."

For Werner, as she was known when she won a Pulitzer for her coverage of the Virginia school integration battle, the memory of how she heard the news is still vivid thirty years later. Benjamin McKelway, the editor of the Washington *Evening Star,* called her in and said sternly that he'd been wrong in hoping the paper would be able to forget about complaints from an integration foe regarding her work. "I was thinking, 'God, what did I do wrong?'" she recalls. Then, shedding his feigned concern, McKelway added, "You see, you have just been awarded a Pulitzer Prize."

Other winners were caught equally by surprise. In 1944, Daniel De Luce, an Associated Press World War II correspondent, was on the beachhead at Anzio, Italy, with an Allied invasion force when Henry Ehrlich, then an army major and later an editor of *Look* magazine, rushed up to deliver the news. "We got some beer out and everybody celebrated," De Luce recalls. Homer Bigart, another war correspondent, was fighting off bedbugs in a third-rate hotel in Warsaw in 1946 when a telegram arrived from the *New York Herald Tribune* informing him that he'd won for his coverage of the Pacific campaign in the closing year of the war. "I was at the bottom," Bigart says of his mood at the time. Celebratory options were few, but the war-torn city had one thing going for it, Bigart recalls: "I ate well—caviar and wonderful vodka—because I had dollars that I could exchange on the black market."

Seattle Times reporter Edwin Guthman was in a vault in Olympia examining government documents in 1950 when he got the word that he'd won for his work in clearing a professor of charges that he had ties to the Communist party. "The AP reporter came running down and said, 'My God, you've won the Pulitzer Prize,' " Guthman recalls. "It came as a total shock. I knew the paper had entered it but I just never thought about it again because it just seemed something so beyond anything that I would ever do.' "

For some journalists, the Pulitzer offers a welcome chance to stop proving oneself. "I could relax," the AP's Daniel De Luce says. "It's like some guy getting into a movie and it's a big, big success. Well, you know, he doesn't have to be a star anymore; he's made it." Others have the opposite reaction. "It makes you feel you have an awful lot to live up to," says *Miami Herald* police reporter Edna Buchanan, who won a Pulitzer in 1986. "Since I won I've even found myself writing two drafts of personal letters."

Gene Miller, also of the *Miami Herald,* says that it was thanks in large part to his first Pulitzer, in 1967, for stories that freed two innocent people jailed for murder, that the Herald gave him the backing and the time—eight and a half years —that he needed to win his second prize for a similar feat. At the same time, though, he says a Pulitzer is a kind of invisible albatross, demanding forever afterward what he calls "a certain level beyond competency." Cartoonist Paul Conrad, who has won three Pulitzers, tells a story of riding up in the *Los Angeles Times* elevator with a copy boy after it had been announced that he'd won a second Pulitzer.

"He said to me, 'Mr. Conrad, which Pulitzer Prize is heavier, the first or the second?' " Conrad recalls. "Isn't that a marvelous question? They do get heavier, because more is expected."

For some reporters, winning a Pulitzer is a turning point in their careers. Edwin Guthman credits his Pulitzer with changing his life, leading to a Nieman fellowship at Harvard and eventually from those contacts to a job with Robert Kennedy and to editorships at major national papers. Still others appreciate the validation that a Pulitzer brings. David Halberstam says that when he and Malcolm Browne of the Associated Press won prizes in 1964 for their reporting in Vietnam, at a time when government officials were strongly criticizing much of the war coverage, "it was if the Supreme Court of our own profession had ruled in our favor."

And even when friends and neighbors don't get quite straight what the prize is all about —Edna Buchanan recalls that after she'd won her Pulitzer, one Miamian, confusing Pulitzer and Nobel, asked her, "Are you going to go to Stockholm to get the prize?"—there is a certain cachet that endures. Pulitzer Prize winners are asked to give commencement speeches, to write books, and to take part on panels to discuss weighty matters like the state of the press. Buchanan, whose byline is much better known than her face, recalls that after she'd won she was interviewed on one of the morning network television shows, complete with limousine pickup. Later that day, she had a further brief taste of stardom when she went to do her grocery shopping in the local supermarket. "Someone recognized me from seeing me on the TV show that morning and said, 'It's really her!' and everybody turned," Buchanan recalls. Even relatives get in on the glory. A 1987 wedding announcement in the *New York Times,* recounting the pedigree of the bride, reported that she was the great-granddaughter of a man who'd won a Pulitzer Prize.

The Pulitzer competition, which now annually draws well over 1500 newspaper entries in more than a dozen categories, wasn't always considered so prestigious. Indeed, in the first ten years after the Pulitzer Prizes started being awarded, there were so few appropriate candidates in the four original categories that the Pulitzer Prize for meritorious public service by a newspaper—the one later won by *the New York Times* for publishing the Pentagon Papers and by the *Washington Post* for its coverage of Watergate—was given only seven times, and the award for excellence in reporting, only nine. (The other categories were editorials and newspaper history, the latter subsequently dropped.) When William "Skeets"

Miller of the Louisville *Courier-Journal* was interviewed after winning a 1926 Pulitzer prize for his reports on a man trapped in a cave, Miller explained that he wasn't even working as a journalist anymore. Instead, he was in the ice cream business with his father and was saving money to go to Europe to study singing.

Editor & Publisher, a major news industry publication, revealed in 1928 that only eighteen stories had been submitted in the reporting category that year, none of which was considered worthy of recognition. The article went on to quote George B. Parker, editorial director of the Scripps-Howard Newspapers, as saying, "In my opinion, all the editors and publishers in the country have shown an astonishing lack of appreciation of the Pulitzer prizes, an institution created in the interests of better American journalism."

Since that precarious beginning, slowly but steadily the Pulitzer Prizes have become a national institution, representing not only a yardstick of excellence in the profession of journalism but also a symbol of the growing power of the press. In a remark that backhandedly acknowledged this state of affairs, then Vice President Spiro Agnew complained at a Republican fund-raising dinner in 1970 that "Pulitzers are not won as quickly exposing the evils of Communism as they are by discrediting an American public official." (Agnew later resigned after pleading guilty to tax fraud, but not as a result of any Pulitzer Prize-winning journalism.) Farther afield, David Halberstam recalls being told by a well-placed Vietnamese friend in the early 1960s, at a time when his reporting was causing particular consternation, that the Saigon government had decided against expelling Halberstam after the friend warned that "If you do that he will win a Pulitzer Prize."

Such recognition would no doubt have brought great pleasure to the founder of the Pulitzer Prizes, Joseph Pulitzer. A driving, dynamic Hungarian who emigrated to America in 1864, Pulitzer first served in the Union army in the Civil War and later settled in St. Louis. In time, he became the owner of papers there and in New York, where his enormously successful *World* developed into the most powerful newspaper of its day. While spearheading the drive to raise enough money to build the base for the Statue of Liberty, the *World* crusaded against monopolies, championed the right of workers to unionize, and fought for social justice. Occasionally, the *World* faltered in its efforts to be a force for the public good, as when it pressed for war with Spain in a fit of competitive fever with William Randolph Hearst. And Pulitzer himself was not without his blind spots, a Victorian attitude toward women and women's suffrage being one of them. But for the most part, the *World* under Pulitzer spoke for the downtrodden and spoke *to* the downtrodden, its circulation rising along with the thundering editorial voice of its founder.

Late in his career, soon after the turn of the century, Pulitzer decided that he wanted to do something to elevate the practice of journalism. He proposed to Columbia University that he give money for a school of journalism and for a set of prizes to reward excellence in the field. "My idea is to recognize that journalism is, or ought to be, one of the great and intellectual professions," Pulitzer wrote at the time. With regard to the prizes, Pulitzer proposed that, once the school was on a solid footing, Columbia should give "annual prizes to particular journalists or writers for various accomplishments, achievements, and forms of excellence." Pulitzer's high hopes are reflected in a letter quoted by retired Pulitzer Prize Board secretary John Hohenberg in his history of the prizes. In that letter, Pulitzer expressed the belief that the prizes "will be of the greatest possible benefit and renown to the university, possibly greater than the school itself."

As Pulitzer envisioned it, and as is still the case, the prizes seek to reward outstanding examples of journalism through an annual competition. The criteria used by the judges emphasize the same qualities valued by Pulitzer, specifying in all categories that preference will be given to work "characterized by high quality of writing and reporting." The early categories have been expanded gradually over the years to include photography and editorial cartoons as well as a variety of reporting categories ranging from international correspondence to feature writing. Now, as then, awards are sometimes made for a single piece of work and sometimes for a series of related pieces. The Pulitzer Prize for public service is based on a newspaper's use of its full journalistic resources, which are now considered to include editorials, cartoons, photographs, and reporting, toward some socially significant end.

As described by Hohenberg, Pulitzer's original proposals were followed by a number of years of squabbling over who was to control the school, with the prizes an adjunct to that quarrel. The eventual outcome was that the school came under the aegis of the university while a group now known as the Pulitzer Prize Board, one of whose members is the president of Columbia and most of the others of whom are high-level news executives, was given prime responsibility for the prizes.

Neither Pulitzer nor the university at first saw any problem in having a board made up almost exclusively of journalists oversee all the awards, which, under terms set down by Pulitzer, include prizes in the arts as well as in journalism. Screening juries made up of experts in their fields choose the music, drama, and literary finalists, but don't pick the actual winners. Predictably, through the years, this arrangement has led to occasional disputes over the quality of the arts judging—although these are probably no more, and quite possibly fewer, than the loud objections that frequently greet the announcement of the journalistic winners. The point has also been made that the Pulitzers don't really function as the top prizes in journalism because they involve only newspapers: magazines, radio, and television are excluded. There seems little likelihood, however, that any fundamental changes will be made in the Pulitzer process.

While TV journalists are not eligible to win Pulitzers, one major reason for the increased recognition of the prizes probably has to do with the glamorization of the news business that those same broadcast journalists have helped to bring about. Thanks to their fame and their medium, all members of the media have been tinged with a Hollywood glow. Another reason may involve the fact that, owing to the emergence of truly national news organizations, the media have come to be seen as increasingly important players in determining the agenda of national debate. What the *New York Times,* the *Wall Street Journal,* and the *Washington Post* choose to display on their front pages has a great deal to do with what Washington politicians and the nation's "elite" will be talking about that day—as well as what will appear on network news shows that night. And then there is the effect of the biggest boost to journalism in recent memory: the fact that the *Washington Post* was responsible for the downfall of a president owing to its exposure of the Watergate affair, a feat that brought the paper a 1973 Pulitzer Prize and that prompted both a popular book and a major movie.

It was of course also the *Washington Post* that was responsible for one of journalism's—and the Pulitzer Prizes'—greatest scandals. In 1981, the *Post* gave back a Pulitzer after ascertaining that reporter Janet Cooke had fabricated her award-winning story about a young heroin addict. That incident led to considerable hand-wringing and public soul-searching, and while it is generally agreed that there was no way the fabrication could have been detected during the judging process, the incident probably hastened some of the reforms in the Pulitzer judging process that have occurred in the past few years.

Osborn Elliott, who was a member of the Pulitzer Prize Board at the time, recalls that the story "had a ring of truth and a verisimilitude that simply didn't cause questions to be raised." And, he adds, "One assumes when you're sitting on a board of that sort that any entry has been fully vetted and reviewed by the submitting paper, particularly when the submitting paper is of the quality of the *Washington Post*." Elliott's comments highlight one aspect of prize-judging that is always fraught with danger: those doing the judging often have no way of knowing just how original, or how accurate, a given entry may be. There has never been another case to match the Janet Cooke incident, but other winning entries have come in for criticism on the grounds either that they have not plowed genuinely new terrain or that they have not accurately portrayed a situation.

Simply because they have existed as long as they have, the Pulitzer Prizes offer a unique perspective on twentieth century history. Cataloguing as they do a succession of wars, domestic disruptions, and instances of venality, the prizes provide ample evidence of the imperfectability of human beings—at least over as short a span as seventy-five years. The prizes also provide some sense of what the American public has been told is significant about the era in which they live.

More than three-hundred Pulitzers have been given out during that period for news stories whose subjects are easily identifiable. Of this total, at least fifty have exposed instances of government corruption or wrongdoing, making it far and away the biggest single category. About the same number have involved other forms of crime or wrongdoing from murder to labor racketeering. Surprisingly, perhaps, given the amount of space newspapers routinely devote to accidents and disasters, only a dozen examples of such coverage have won Pulitzer Prizes. More than a dozen prizes each have gone to stories involving science and race issues.

Acknowledging a major reality of the twentieth century, stories about war and upheaval have won more than thirty prizes. And reflecting a preoccupation with the Soviet Union, a dozen Pulitzers have gone to stories about Russia and Eastern Europe. By contrast, Western Europe, Africa, and the Middle East have each accounted for about half that number.

Certainly one of the strongest threads that run through the lives and reminiscences of Pulitzer winners is that of coping with an American antipathy toward Moscow that at times has translated into suspicion of anyone who is not actively anti-Communist. Walter Duranty and the *New*

York Times parted company in the 1930s, after Duranty had won a Pulitzer for his reporting on Russia, following years of criticism inside and outside the paper regarding what Duranty's critics viewed as his overly sympathetic portrayal of the Soviet system. In the early days of what came to be known as the McCarthy era, reporter Edwin Guthman was publicly accused in the Washington State legislature of "taking the *Seattle Times* for a ride in a little Red Wagon" for his efforts to look into charges of pro-communism directed at local people. As late as the 1960s, Vietnam War correspondent David Halberstam recalls, *New York Times* editors who had lived through the McCarthy period remained skittish about any story or sentiment that could be perceived as pro-communist.

The issue of race in America is another theme that runs through the seventy-five-year history of the Pulitzer Prizes, from the Columbus (Ga.) *Enquirer Sun*'s editorials against lynching in the twenties to the *Boston Globe*'s series examining race relations in Boston in the eighties. While the number of stories specifically focusing on race is not large, many other reports have underlying racial elements. Whether exposing instances of wrongful imprisonment or inhuman conditions in a mental hospital, examples of racially-linked injustice are so numerous as to lead to the conclusion that bigotry and discrimination are woven deeply into every aspect of twentieth century American life.

If a survey of the history of the prizes shows what subjects have been most showered with prizes in the past seventy-five years, so, too, does it show what news organizations have most often been honored. The *New York Times* has won about sixty Pulitzers out of a total of six hundred or so Pulitzer journalism prizes given out, reflecting the fact that it has been the dominant national paper of this century. Similarly, the Associated Press, the dominant national wire service, has won three dozen awards, split about evenly between photography and news stories. No other news organization has come close to these two giants, but among those that had won at least a dozen awards by the end of the 1980s are the *Washington Post*, the *Boston Globe*, the *Des Moines Register and Tribune*, the *Los Angeles Times*, the *St. Louis Post-Dispatch*, the *Philadelphia Inquirer*, the *Wall Street Journal*, and the *Chicago Tribune*.

In fairness, it should be noted that while there is evidence that the Pulitzer Prize Board bends over backward to give awards to small papers, the fact is that big papers have a better shot at Pulitzers because they have the resources to win them. That means both good people and plenty of money. Rick Reiff, who was a reporter for the *Akron Beacon Journal* when that paper won a Pulitzer in 1987 for its coverage of a takeover battle between Goodyear Tire and Rubber Company and Sir James Goldsmith, later remarked in the *Business Journalist* that the paper's seriousness about the story even extended to not quibbling about paying overtime, which he described as "a touchy subject at the *Beacon*." Reiff went on to say, "In a crude way, all the expenses reflect the commitment that won the *Beacon Journal* a Pulitzer. You want a shot at the prize, buddy? Ante up a few thousand dollars and you get to play. Many papers lose before they start."

Pulitzer Prize-winning stories have at times been genuinely daring and at others have set standards of excellence that have affected the whole profession. In the 1920s, for example, two Southern newspapers were cited for their fearless reporting on the Klan. The *New York Times'* 1972 prize for publishing the Pentagon Papers, followed the next year by the *Washington Post*'s prize for its coverage of Watergate, not only exposed government secrets and wrongdoing, but also inspired a whole generation of young journalists to dig below the surface of events. While newspapers occasionally seem preoccupied with winning Pulitzers, it can also be argued that thanks to the Pulitzer incentive, news organizations sometimes support far higher quality journalism than might otherwise be the case.

Over the years prizes have gone to reporters who risked their lives in the line of duty, among them correspondent Ernie Pyle, who died during a battle in the Pacific shortly before the end of World War II. They have also gone to newspapers and individuals who have risked their publications' livelihood in order to speak the truth as they saw it—people like Albert Scardino, who recalls that in the darkest financial days of the *Georgia Gazette,* when the weekly he had started with his wife was faced with what amounted to an advertising boycott, "We could never get beyond thinking that if we don't publish a story in order to survive then what's the point, there's no reason for us to be here."

Pulitzers have gone to young cubs like James Mulroy and Alvin Goldstein, both barely into their twenties, who won in 1925 for dogged reporting that helped to solve the Loeb-Leopold murder case; and to only modestly more established pros like Seymour Hersh, whose equally dogged efforts led to his winning a prize in 1970 for exposing the My Lai massacre in Vietnam. Most extraordinary, perhaps, is the fact that more than two dozen individual Pulitzer Prize winners, including cartoonists and photographers as well as reporters, have won more than one award.

But if there is much to admire about the Pulitzers, there is also no lack of instances in which journalistic judgments or procedures have been questioned. *Time* magazine caustically noted in 1923 that Alva Johnston of the *New York Times,* the winner of the Pulitzer Prize for the best reportorial work in the previous year, "did not expose a great graft ring, did not describe a great national catastrophe, did not report a momentous political event, made no great 'scoop.' What he reported was a convention of the American Association for the Advancement of Science in Cambridge, Mass." (In fairness to Johnston, his reports were careful accounts of scientific issues.) In 1932, the Pulitzer Prize Board awarded a reporting prize to five staff members of the *Detroit Free Press* for their gripping coverage of—an American Legion parade. In 1944, the *New York Times* was honored with a Pulitzer Prize for public service for a survey—suggested by a member of the owning family—that revealed the earthshaking fact that college students had a poor knowledge of American history.

At a deeper level, Pulitzer Prize-winning stories, taken as a whole, have generally done a poor job—as has journalism in general—of seeing the forest as well as the trees. While often brilliantly reporting on day-to-day events, newspapers have failed to grasp and illuminate many of the sweeping trends and underlying realities of succeeding eras. In the 1930s, to judge by the Pulitzer winners, the most serious issue facing the country was municipal fraud, not the Great Depression or widespread calls for radical economic and political change. In the 1960s, Pulitzers were awarded for coverage of racial riots and their aftermath, but no paper won a prize for a story explaining the rise of black power. In the 1970s and 1980s there were prizewinning reports on scams of every sort imaginable, from the pulpit to Wall Street, but there was no prizewinning series that limned the outlines of the fledgling women's movement or that focused on the rise of the gay movement. Despite all the talk in journalistic circles about newspapers getting away from covering breaking news as television took over, and becoming instead more interpretive and broader in perspective, the stories that won Pulitzer Prizes seemed on the whole remarkably similar in subject matter and approach to those that had gone before.

To understand at least one reason why this has been so, one need look no further than the pictures of Pulitzer judges preserved in the Pulitzer archives —a dusty room perched above the Columbia Journalism School library. The early photos show a succession of well-fed looking gentlemen, all of them white, most of them middle-aged or beyond, perusing Pulitzer entries or sitting for formal portraits with an air of high moral rectitude. They are members of a club, the pictures seem to suggest, not just leaders in their own institutions but in the world at large. At some point, the pictures start to change: a couple of black faces appear, a couple of women. The pocket watches disappear, along with some of the wrinkles. But they don't change all that much, and they don't change all that fast.

That reality, and the continuing reality of who occupies the top seats in American newsrooms, are not lost even on those one-time outsiders who have been invited to join the club. "News in this country is what a group of middle-aged, middle-class white men say it is," says former Pulitzer Prize Board chairman Roger Wilkins. "They have in fact participated in a very narrow slice of the human experience and yet they behave as if it is the standard American experience and the standard human experience. So that when, for example, a woman comes and sits down at the table the reaction is that her vision, since it is different, is deficient. When a black sits down at the table the same thing is true. I wish I had had the wit of one black journalist who said, 'My editor is always telling me that my vision is clouded by my blackness. It never occurs to him that his vision is clouded by his whiteness.' "

Writing in [More] magazine in 1972, John McCormally foreshadowed Wilkins' comments in a recollective essay that described his recent service as a member of a Pulitzer screening jury as a vain search for fresh voices or vision. By the middle of the first day, wrote McCormally, then editor of the Burlington (Iowa) Hawk Eye, he began to understand why. "The commitment to Victorian convention was confirmed beyond doubt when we adjourned at twelve-fifteen for lunch with Columbia President William J. McGill in the Men's Faculty Club," McCormally wrote. "Men's Faculty Club, indeed. But then, why not? There were no women on the Pulitzer juries . . . We did include Moses Newsom of the Afro-American Newspapers, so we weren't lily-white, as I'd begun to fear. But here we were, the lesser elite of the American press, come to honor the best among us, and we were totally male—more than a half century after women's suffrage and well into the era of women's liberation."

Whether because of a lack of women and minorities in American newsrooms, or because of unconscious bias in the judging itself, white men totally dominated among prizewinners until the 1980s. Through 1979, only about twenty women and people of color were to be found among

about four hundred named winners. (These numbers do not take account
of individuals who may have been part of prizewinning teams whose
members were not individually named.)

By the end of the 1980s, minorities still accounted for less than 8
percent of newsroom professionals, and women, while reasonably well
represented in the reporting ranks, still were scarce at the upper levels.
But by then, a quarter of the Pulitzer jurors, and a third of the Pulitzer
Prize Board members, were women or people of color. The composition
of the Pulitzer winners changed, too: during the decade of the 1980s, more
than thirty named Pulitzer Prize winners were "nonstandard Americans,"
as Wilkins terms them—one-and-a-half times the entire number up to
that time. "What more prizes being won by minorities and women shows
is that, with equal opportunity, black people and women will get the jobs
and they will win the prizes," says Robert C. Maynard, publisher and
editor of the Oakland (Calif.) *Tribune* and a member of the Pulitzer Prize
Board. But what can never be known is how much more quickly the
makeup of American newsrooms might have changed, and with it the
industry's reporting on a whole range of issues, not just those relating to
race and gender, if the choices of judges and prizewinners had provided
earlier evidence that women and minorities, and their work, were valued
at the highest levels of their profession.

If the clubby nature of the Pulitzer process helped to shut out women
and minorities for many years, it also, at times, shut out those whose view
of the news did not find favor with the establishment—that invisible but
real institution whose leadership includes the pooh-bahs of the Fourth
Estate. In 1967, Harrison Salisbury of the *New York Times,* who had
already won a Pulitzer for his coverage of Russia in the 1950s, was selected
by a Pulitzer screening jury as its first choice for his reports from Communist North Vietnam. Some Pulitzer Prize Board members claimed later
that they simply found Salisbury's reporting not up to prize standards
when it came time to choose a winner. In his memoirs, retired *Times*
executive editor Turner Catledge, who at the time of the Salisbury flap
was a member of the Pulitzer Prize Board, offered another explanation. As
he recalled it, he was present, but abstaining, when the board "narrowly
voted against giving the Pulitzer Prize to Salisbury. I was terribly upset by
this vote, because I was convinced that several of my colleagues made
their decision on political rather than journalistic grounds; indeed they
made no bones about it. They supported the war, so they voted against
Salisbury."

But for all of Catledge's distress over the Salisbury affair, the fact is that the *New York Times* was at least part of the club, membership in which has proven to have its value. *Los Angeles Times* media critic David Shaw noted in a study of the Pulitzer process contained in his 1984 book *Press Watch* that the *Baltimore Sun* won nine Pulitzers from 1928 to 1953 while its editor, Frank Kent, was on the Pulitzer Prize Board, but didn't win a single Pulitzer in the first twenty-five years after Kent left the board. Similarly, Shaw found that in the twenty-five years that Kent Cooper of the Associated Press served on the board (1931–1956), AP won fourteen Pulitzers and its rival, United Press, not a single one. The year after Cooper left the board, UP, later UPI, won its first Pulitzer.

Again, as in the case of race and gender, things have changed enormously in recent years. For example, a later study by Shaw showed that between 1970 and 1983, 90 percent of the Pulitzer finalists came from the Eastern papers. Between 1984 and 1988, at a time when the composition of the Pulitzer screening juries was becoming more geographically balanced, that figure dropped to 65 percent. In 1990, seven out of fifteen Pulitzer Prizes went to Western papers. But even given such dramatic shifts, certain realities persist. As one board member puts it, you can't help the fact that you read certain papers and talk to certain people. In 1990, the members of the Pulizer Prize Board included representatives of thirteen newspapers. Among them were the *New York Times,* the *Washington Post,* the *Los Angeles Times,* the *Philadelphia Inquirer,* and the Oakland *Tribune*—all of which papers also won 1990 Pulitzer Prizes.

The actual judging of the Pulitzer journalism prizes is a fairly straightforward matter. The process is overseen by a staff of three people who work in a small office tucked away in a top-floor corner of Columbia's Journalism Building. By the beginning of each judging season, they have received and catalogued so many Pulitzer journalism entries that just lugging the stacks of scrapbooks to the rooms where they will be judged is a major undertaking. Although the contest draws a few hopefuls who paste their own stories together and fill out the required cover sheets, in practice submissions are usually made by news organizations rather than by individuals.

Each year about sixty editors and a sprinkling of reporters and others are chosen to be members of screening juries that evaluate these submissions. The juries gather at Columbia for three days and pass their selected finalists on to the Pulitzer Prize Board. At one time, the juries routinely ranked their finalists, but this is no longer the case.

The eighteen-member Pulitzer Prize Board, primarily editors and publishers with a more recent smattering of reporters, columnists and academics, makes the final decisions at Columbia a few weeks later. The board has the right to move finalists from one category to another or to disregard the juries' choices altogether. The board also selects new board members and new members of the screening juries, generally from names suggested by current or past participants in the process. Members of the journalism juries and of the Pulitzer Prize Board are not paid for their services.

Formerly, the Columbia University trustees had the right to accept the board's choices or, as an alternative, to withhold the prize in any category. After several acrimonious years during which some trustees objected to giving prizes to, among others, the *New York Times* for printing the Pentagon Papers and columnist Jack Anderson for writing about American policy decision-making during the Indo-Pakistan War of 1971, on the grounds that both involved the publication of secret government documents, the trustees removed themselves entirely from the prize-giving process in 1975.

In the course of the exchanges leading up to that move, Columbia President McGill told the *Columbia Spectator,* the campus daily, that his personal opinion was that journalists shouldn't get any awards for what he perceived as violating the law. "The newspaper profession has to discipline itself," McGill said. "I don't think the profession pays enough attention to matters of repercussions—they are a very hard-bitten type of people."

Just how one judges excellence, and who should make that determination, remains a subject of discussion. Joseph Pulitzer himself urged that the Pulitzer Prize Board include nonjournalists, but his suggestion was ignored after his death. In his 1972 essay on his service as a Pulitzer juror, John McCormally wrote that Pulitzer juries should add not just women, minorities, and younger people, but also "some nonpress critics of the press to make the process more representative of and responsive to the most vital forces at work in the society. Somewhere among the jurors or advisers there ought to be room for a [Ralph] Nader, a Jesse Jackson, a Walter Hickel, a Saul Alinsky, a Gloria Steinem or an F. Lee Bailey; maybe even a Spiro Agnew and a Daniel Berrigan—people able not only to concede what the press is capable of doing, but also recognize what it doesn't do."

The Pulitzer Prize Board agreed at the beginning of the 1980s that up to three nonjournalists could be appointed to its ranks, but through the 1980s only one true nonjournalist—not counting the Columbia president—served at any given time. "It's impossible for the nonjournalist to have any real grasp of the ethical issue involved, the technical expertise needed, the ways that journalists go about their work," says former board member Osborn Elliott, by way of explaining what appears to be a general lack of enthusiasm for any proposal such as that put forth by McCormally. "I think that's in part because of the lousy job journalism does in explaining itself."

The judging of the Pulitzers begins in late winter with meetings of the five-person screening juries. The juries are installed in unused rooms and faculty offices throughout Columbia's Journalism School, with several assigned to the "World Room," so named for the ornately carved chairs and massive stained glass window depicting the Statue of Liberty that once were part of the furnishings of Pulitzer's *World.* (The paper merged in 1931 with the *New York Telegram,* now defunct.) As in McCormally's time, the jurors break for lunch, but now they go to the simply named Faculty House, and some of them pause to comb their hair in the ladies' room before they ascend to the upper floor of the gracious old building overlooking Morningside Park.

The scene in the cavernous World Room late on a gloomy February afternoon during one recent Pulitzer judging was in full accord with Pulitzer's sense of the high-minded seriousness of his prizes. Everywhere, on chairs, tables, and floors, were vast piles of scrapbooks containing the year's entries. In one corner, a couple of jurors were deep in conversation; in another, tired-looking members of a group that hadn't even broken for lunch were still in the process of reading the more than 100 entries in their category. At one time, every member of a screening jury read every entry, but by the beginning of the 1990s, growing numbers of entries had caused some juries to devise ways of more rapidly winnowing their piles.

If the Pulitzer judging process seemed lacking in the glamor suggested by its name, the jurors didn't seem to mind. In fact, most said it was fun and some even thought it was a valuable experience. "You see what works and what doesn't," David Anable, former managing editor of the *Christian Science Monitor,* commented in the midst of his first stint as a juror. "I have to think that if you consider the effect on everyone who has been a juror over the years this process has had a great influence on American journalism." David Shaw, the *Los Angeles Times* media critic, said that after two years as a juror, he was "very impressed by how open-minded people were. I was required to be out of the room at one point while the group was discussing an entry from my paper and when I came back I heard two people discussing how each had changed the other's mind."

Pulitzer Prize Board members are no less enthusiastic about their task. "It's delicious, enlightening, and educational," says Robert Maynard of the Oakland *Tribune*. It's also, he says, "an awesome responsibility." Maynard's praise is itself an indication of much the prize-giving process has changed. In 1981, as a member of a screening jury whose feature-writing candidates had all been rejected by the Pulitzer Board in order to give the prize to Janet Cooke, Maynard reacted angrily to the ensuing debacle. Describing himself as "mad because I traveled 3,000 miles from my newspaper, spent three days sitting on my tail getting saddle sores, reading 160 submissions," Maynard was quoted as having called the selection process "an obnoxious travesty and a thorough waste of people's time." These days, Maynard says, when any questions arise at the board level, "the juries are consulted."

For those individuals and newspapers who withstand all the rigors—and vagaries—of the Pulitzer competition and finally survive to claim their prizes, the actual rewards are relatively modest. Each Pulitzer Prize winner gets a check for $3,000 (raised from $1,000 in the late 1980s) and a citation; in the case of the prize for public service, the paper gets a gold medal suitable for putting in a sock drawer. Through most of their history, the prizes were simply sent off through the mail. Starting in the early 1980s, however, they were presented at a lunch at Columbia by the president of Columbia, Michael Sovern, who joked that Columbia had decided that the empty feeling some prizewinners experienced after they'd won their Pulitzers was in reality just hunger.

There is rarely any speech-making at these events; the winners, almost always looking ill-at-ease, shake hands and hurry back to their seats. For their employers, though, a Pulitzer is reason to crow. And crow. Full-page ads in industry publications and elsewhere trumpet the achievements of a winning paper's staff, and potential advertisers and subscribers are fully apprised of a paper's claims to Pulitzer fame. Even years later, a single Pulitzer, like a single positive restaurant review, continues to be cherished. John D. Paulson, retired editor of the Fargo (N.D.) *Forum*, recalled in the late 1980s that, based on the *Forum*'s one prize for coverage of a tornado thirty years before, the paper still referred to itself as a Pulitzer Prize-winning newspaper.

There is some reason to be concerned that newspapers have become almost too enamored of the idea of winning Pulitzers. Joe Hughes was a member of the San Diego *Evening Tribune* staff responsible for the paper's Pulitzer Prize-winning coverage of an airliner crash in 1979, the first such prize the paper had ever won. Says Hughes, "We didn't think much about Pulitzers in those days. Since then, of course, we think about them all the time and we write what we call news packages that are designed to attract attention." The *Tribune* is hardly alone. Reporters and editors around the country tell of meetings to plot Pulitzer strategy and readers occasionally voice the suspicion that some multipart series or other is aimed not at them but at capturing the attention of a prize judge. Good as such productions often are, there may be something wrong when a *Newsday* editor brags that a series he oversaw, and that won a Pulitzer Prize, had to be cut down in order to fit into a book. Or when Pulitzer Prize Board member James Hoge, Jr., publisher of the New York *Daily News,* is led to comment that after two days of judging Pulitzers, "I'm inclined to say that news is pathology and news is very, very long."

Still, even with regard to how much effort they expend in trying to win a prize, newspapers of the late part of the century are not so different from those of earlier years. One prizewinning behemoth entered by the *Detroit Free Press* in 1945 is contained in a nineteen-pound scrapbook whose cover is embossed in gold, making it probably the heaviest if not the weightiest Pulitzer entry in history. Similarly, the series on Germany for which Herbert Bayard Swope won his Pulitzer in 1917 contained no fewer than nineteen installments—as seemingly interminable now as they must have appeared to at least some readers then.

As for trying to tailor coverage to win a Pulitzer, board member Robert Maynard argues that any paper trying to discern a pattern in Pulitzer awards will almost certainly fail. "Journalism is dynamic, not static," he says. "The very fact that something wins one year means it probably won't win the next."

As the Pulitzer Prizes move toward the twenty-first century, there is reason to think that while the need for further reforms in journalism remains critical, the prizes will continue to reward excellence and to uphold the crusading tradition of Joseph Pulitzer's newspapers. In 1989, *Atlanta Journal and Constitution* reporter Bill Dedman won a Pulitzer for his investigation of the racial discrimination practiced by commercial banks and savings-and-loan institutions in Atlanta. In 1990, the *Washington* (N.C.) *Daily News,* with an editorial staff of only nine people, won a public service medal for revealing not only that the municipal water supply was contaminated but also that local officials had known that fact for years.

There is also every reason to think that in the future, as in the past, a phone call in some distant city to inform a winner of her prize, or a message appearing on a reporter's video screen, will produce a moment so thrilling that, as one prizewinner described it, the only thing that could compare was the birth of his children.

Years later, those future winners will sit down like David Halberstam over a cup of coffee in his New York apartment, or like Homer Bigart over a cup of tea in his New Hampshire farmhouse, and they will get to talking about how they got into journalism in the first place, and how they worked their way up to a foreign assignment or just happened to be in the city room the night of the big story, and they will joke a little, and smile at their foolish bravery or their luck, and remember.

What follows is an excerpt from the first article in Swope's Pulitzer Prize-winning series on Germany, and then a brief passage from a preface that Swope wrote in 1949 to a book entitled *A Treasury of Great Reporting*, edited by Louis L. Snyder and Richard B. Morris, which gives some insight into Swope's journalistic philosophy.

PART

I

THE EARLY YEARS

□

1

HERBERT BAYARD SWOP

Germany During World War

IN THE LATE TEENS AND 1920S, IT MUST HAVE SE
many people that Herbert Bayard Swope *was* journalism in Ar
as one of the star reporters at the *World,* and eventually a
editor, Swope conferred with mayors, dined with movie stars, a
presidents. Tall and red-haired, with a penchant for fast horse:
clothes, Swope cut a dashing figure in New York and elsewhere
personification of all that was glamorous in the years leading
Great Depression.

But while Swope was leading a life filled with parties a
placed friends, he was also infusing the *World* with new vigor a
tion. Under his guidance, the *World* reached the peak of its in
power, giving a forum to some of the most lively voices of the p
the *World*'s op-ed page. At the same time, the paper continued t
pion social justice in forms including an attack on the Ku Klux K
won the paper a Pulitzer Prize in 1922.

Swope had led the way with his own Pulitzer Prize for repor
1917, when he was thirty-five. Swope's award, the first of its kin
given, came for an evenhanded series of stories on Germany reporte
written before America's entry into the First World War. Subsequ
the articles were published as a book, *Inside the German Empire.* S
never wrote his memoirs, so all that remains of his German exploit
the reports themselves, together with such additions as he made in
book.

In later life, Swope ran his own public relations and public pc
consulting firm, while remaining an intimate of leading politicians
corporate executives of his day. According to Swope biographer E. J. Ka
Jr., Swope took a personal interest in the Pulitzer Prizes for the rest of
life and routinely sent notes of congratulation to new winners.

THE WORLD
November 4, 1916

GERMANY KEEN FOR PEACE, BUT EXPECTS AND IS READY TO BATTLE ON FOR YEARS
by
HERBERT BAYARD SWOPE

The desire for peace is strong in Germany, but from top to bottom there is no belief that it is near. German hopes and expectations of the end are indefinite as to time—the most optimistic can see no real prospects within another two years, and from that period the conjectures run up to ten years. And in their economic and military planning the Kaiser's subjects are preparing to enact their motto of "durchalten" (stick it out) for years to come.

As a striking illustration of how far away is the idea of any peace that Germany herself does not make, I can submit this news of secret diplomacy, which may meet denial, but which is unqualifiedly true: Within the last eighteen months no fewer than eleven separate interrogatories have been submitted to the German Government as to Belgium. The question has been asked by the United States, Spain, Denmark, Holland, Sweden, Switzerland, Norway and other neutrals, if Germany will give a formal assurance of the restoration of Belgian entity at the end of the war—and *not once has this assurance been given,* nor has the Kaiser's Government, in its most affable moments, permitted even inferentially the idea to gain ground that it regarded Belgium's reestablishment according to the status quo ante as an essential.

In some notes I prepared for submission to the Chancellor, regarding the objectives of the war (to which reference is made further on in this article) the suggestion that Belgium would be re-erected within her old lines was carefully blue-pencilled by an official acting for the Chancellor. The explanation was made that Belgium was, as Kaiser Wilhelm I said in a letter to his Empress, a point of weakness, in the empire's rear and flank. Therefore, Germany must be safeguarded against this danger.

HERBERT BAYARD SWOPE:
THE STORY BEHIND THE STORY

From the Preface to *A Treasury of Great Reporting*

I have been a newspaperman all my life, and a reporter during a large period of my activity. Once when I was so fortunate as to be a guest of Kipling, he said that a good reporter was the noblest work of God; that he wanted always to be known as a reporter. . . .

I think too much emphasis these days is laid upon good writing instead of good getting. There are too many press agents who substitute for the reporter. And in the truer function of the reporter—swarming all over the story and making it wholly his—we had men who made journalistic history. No poll parrots they—no mere echoes of the songs sung by hired hands. They always insisted on seeing the central figure. If not, they would know the reason why! They refused to take "No!" for an answer. And they turned first to the "morgue"—an important step in any story. But it is a practice not always followed today.

That was the best method of obtaining accuracy—the prize element of good journalism. And that quality has been distorted and smeared by those who write with no pretense at verification. . . .

If I were stood up against a wall and compelled to answer as to what is the greatest characteristic of good journalism, I would say with my one-time chief [Joseph Pulitzer]:

"Accuracy, terseness, accuracy." And I would add, as an afterthought, "Accuracy."

2

ALVIN H. GOLDSTEIN AND
JAMES W. MULROY
The Loeb–Leopold Murder Case

ALVIN GOLDSTEIN AND JAMES MULROY WERE "CUB REPORT-
ers" at the *Chicago Daily News* in 1924 when Robert Franks, the teenage
son of a wealthy manufacturer, was kidnapped and murdered. Thanks in
large part to the pairs' sleuthing, which turned up a series of fresh facts,
the murderers were caught within ten days. They turned out to be two
wealthy young students, Richard Loeb and Nathan Leopold, whose "thrill"
crime horrified and fascinated the nation.

Mulroy and Goldstein were awarded a Pulitzer Prize for their efforts.
Following is a *Daily News* story that was based on their locating the
typewriter on which a ransom note had been written and a later *News*
article telling how Mulroy and Goldstein had gone about their work.

CHICAGO DAILY NEWS
May 30, 1924

LEOPOLD TYPEWRITER FRANKS CASE CLUE

Evidence that Nathan Leopold, Jr., wealthy 19-year-old "prodigy," owns a portable typewriter, with characteristics amazingly like those of the machine used by the kidnaper of young Robert Franks, was found to-day by a reporter for The Daily News.

The evidence was regarded as the most important link in a chain of circumstances in which young Leopold figures. . . .

The typewriter find was made through law-class notes, given by Leopold to a fellow-student, who had expected to clear his friend by producing them.

"Sure, I have stuff that Leopold typed," said the friend. "In fact, I can give you examples from both of his typewriters."

Leopold had been insisting all through a night and day of questioning that he owned only one machine, a Hammond. The friend produced examples from two typewriters, one the Hammond and the other apparently a portable.

A typewriter expert was summoned into consultation by the police. After a microscopic examination of both samples, he tentatively announced that he thought one machine had produced both.

Samples and expert were then taken to the state's attorney's office by Capt. William Schumaker, so that Leopold might be confronted.

In several points, scarcely discernible by the casual reader but as big as monuments to the expert, the kidnaper's $10,000 ransom letter, written to Jacob Franks after the murder, and the typed class notes seemed the same.

Peculiar type faces made it easily apparent that the two specimens had been done on machines of identical make and model. In addition a slightly off-line "t" and a minutely twisted "i" seemed to make the comparison still more intimate.

Typewriters have peculiarities no less marked than handwritings, according to experts. Examination of the two samples under a microscope was expected to give either a final answer to the kidnaping or a new alibi for the college student.

GOLDSTEIN AND MULROY:
THE STORY BEHIND THE STORY

CHICAGO DAILY NEWS
May 31, 1924

CUB REPORTERS WIN FRANKS CASE GLORY

Two "cub" reporters of The Daily News staff—James Mulroy and Alvin H. Goldstein—contributed more than most of the police force and the legions of rival newsmen combined to the solution of the Franks kidnapping mystery.

"O'Connor and Goldberg," their scornful rivals called them—a wheeze inspired by the almost fanatic zeal with which Mulroy and Goldstein wore out shoe leather in their search for clews. "O'Connor and Goldberg" they may be till they're gray and reading the copy of cubs yet unborn, but the names will be service medals, not taunts. Nobody's kidding the pair to-day.

It's a story of a story—a perfect realization of the dreams of all the thousands of cubs who come stumbling into the dusty local rooms of all the newspapers of the land, green and unskilled and ambitious. To jump from picture-chasing to triumph over the whole town in the biggest story of a generation sounds like the poppycock of newspaper fiction, but "O'Connor and Goldberg" did it.

They dug up the truth about the kidnaping before any one but friends of the Franks family knew about it. They accomplished a scoop which would have given most reporters glory enough for a lifetime when they brought about identification of the kidnaped boy's body a full jump ahead of every other newspaper in Chicago. They ran and taxied and poked about day and night through the week of frenzy that followed, turning up valuable information under the noses of the police and their rivals.

All unaided, they got the evidence that broke the kidnapers' resistance to-day. "O'Connor and Goldberg" solved the mystery, if anybody did. Without them it might have remained a mystery forever.

Ten days ago they were legging it over town, hunting pictures, getting statements from press bureaus, checking up on minor details that real reporters didn't have time for. A good-natured, breezy pair, doing the dreary routine that lies back of the news. Nobody paid much attention to them; they were just a pair of cubs.

Mulroy was sitting in a back corner of the local room of The Daily News office, killing time, on the morning of Wednesday, May 21, when a "tip" came in about a kidnaping "that Sam Ettelson knows all about." He was sent to see Ettelson.

Now Ettelson wasn't anxious to have the newspapers get hold of the fact that the 14-year-old son of his old friend, Jacob Franks, had been kidnaped. But Mulroy has the priceless kind of personality that can't be resisted—the kind that's worth a Rolls-Royce income in the bond business. He talked the story out of Ettelson.

The story wasn't printed. Publication might imperil the life of the kidnaped boy. But Mulroy didn't let that bother him. He got his pal Goldstein and they set to work.

Goldstein was sent hustling out to Hegewisch, where the body of an unidentified boy had been found, crammed naked into a railroad culvert. Mulroy went out to the Franks home.

The description Goldstein phoned to Mulroy at the Franks house apparently didn't fit the kidnaped boy. Eyeglasses had been found near the Hegewisch body and young Franks never had worn glasses.

The Franks couldn't be interested at first, but at last Goldstein and Mulroy got an uncle of the missing boy into a taxicab, headed for the Hegewisch morgue.

The activities of "O'Connor and Goldberg" had caused Ettelson to phone to the city editor of another afternoon paper by this time lest the story leak into print there, and a reporter for that paper horned in on the ride to the morgue. But he wasn't a match for the relentless cubs. They ran circles around him and had the news of the identification into their office an edition ahead of their winded rival.

Well, a kidnaping-murder was too good a story for a pair of cubs, of course. Veterans were assigned to the case. Every newspaper in town, including The Daily News, put its best talent to work on the mystery—big-leaguers.

Goldstein and Mulroy? Oh they just stuck. "Leggers" were needed, and anyhow they would have refused to leave the job. They are reported to have slept and eaten in relays, so that one of them would be on the case if anything happened.

Day and night they were at it, never sitting still. Hunting them by telephone was a mystery in itself. One minute they'd be at the Franks home, almost next minute one of them would bob up at a police station, and the other on some mysterious errand they had no time to explain, off in some other sector of the field of action.

Thus they canvassed all of East 63rd street until they located the drug store which was to have been the kidnapers' rendezvous with Franks —an important find.

Also in the course of their investigations they bumped into young Loeb and incidentally got from him a chance statement that proved of great value later.

"If I was going to kill any kid," said Loeb to Goldstein, "I'd pick just such a fresh little—as that Franks kid."

Yesterday saw their supreme triumph. While rival reporters and detectives were pounding their skulls for a hunch on Leopold and Loeb, Goldstein and Mulroy went out to the University of Chicago campus and scouted about until they had found samples of typewriting done by Leopold on the very typewriter that produced the kidnapers' ransom letter.

They turned the stuff over to the police (after reporting their scoop, of course) and then, still forgetting sleep, they rounded up four college witnesses who popped into the case along about midnight to break down the alibis and the nerve of the two kidnapers.

They were there at the Criminal court building all night and they were still on the job at daybreak with volumes of exclusive material for their paper's first edition.

They're at it somewhere (maybe chasing pictures again) as this is written. They'll get their sleep when the excitement dies down and the paper doesn't need their help.

3

WILLIAM BURKE MILLER
Trapped in a Kentucky Cave

IN 1925, A MAN NAMED FLOYD COLLINS WAS TRAPPED AND injured while exploring a sandstone cave in Kentucky. The unsuccessful seventeen-day effort to rescue him, which was followed by people throughout the country, was chronicled by a young Louisville *Courier-Journal* reporter named William Burke "Skeets" Miller. Miller, who weighed only 110 pounds, was able to wiggle down a narrow passageway to reach Collins, but was unable to free him.

Following is a portion of one of the sequence of stories on the rescue attempt for which Miller won a Pulitzer Prize. It is followed by an article in the New York *World* that appeared after the Pulitzer winners were announced, describing Miller and his exploits. Miller, who at the time did not intend to remain in journalism, later worked for NBC.

THE LOUISVILLE COURIER-JOURNAL
February 3, 1925

COLLINS STILL HOPES FOR LIFE
by
WILLIAM BURKE MILLER

Cave City, Ky., Feb. 2 —Floyd Collins is suffering torture almost beyond description, but he still is hopeful he will be taken out alive, he told me at 6:20 o'clock tonight on my last visit to him.

Until I went inside myself I could not understand exactly what the situation was. I wondered why someone couldn't do something quick, but I found out why.

I was lowered by my heels into the entrance of Sand Cave. The passage way is about five feet in diameter. After reaching the end of an eighty-foot drop I reached fairly level ground for a moment.

From here on I had to squirm like a snake. Water covers almost every inch of the ground, and after the first few feet I was wet through and through. Every moment it got colder. It seemed that I would crawl forever, but after going about ninety feet I reached a very small compartment, slightly larger than the remainder of the channel.

This afforded a breathing spell before I started again on toward the prisoner. The dirty water splashed in my face and numbed my body, but I couldn't stop.

Finally I slid down an eight-foot drop and, a moment later, saw Collins and called to him. He mumbled an answer.

My flashlight revealed a face on which is written suffering of many long hours, because Collins has been in agony every conscious moment since he was trapped at 10 o'clock Friday morning. I saw the purple of his lips, the pallor on the face, and realized that something must be done before long if this man is to live.

Before I could see his face, however, I was forced to raise a small piece of oil cloth covering it.

"Put it back," he said. "Put it back—the water."

Then I noticed a small drip-drip-drip from above. Each drop struck Collins' face. The first few hours he didn't mind, but the constant dripping almost drove him insane. His brother had taken the oil cloth to him earlier in the day.

This reminded me of the old water torture used in ages past. I shuddered. . . .

Homer Collins had brought with him some body harness to place around his brother, and we finally succeeded in putting it on him.

The prisoner helped as best he could by squirming and turning as much as possible, and finally we were ready to haul away on the rope attached to Collins. We pulled as much as we could and it seemed as though we made headway. It was estimated we moved the prisoner five inches.

Perhaps we did, but I can hardly realize it. All of us were on the point of collapse and after a short time our strength failed. We couldn't do any more.

We saw that the blankets and covering which Collins' brother had brought to him were in place and that he was resting as comfortably as we could make him.

Then we left near his head a lantern well filled with oil. It isn't much, but the tiny light it throws means much in that relentless trap and it may bring some bit of consolation to a daring underground explorer whose chance for life is small.

WILLIAM BURKE MILLER:
THE STORY BEHIND THE STORY

THE WORLD
May 4, 1926

William Burke Miller, winner of the Pulitzer Prize for the best example of a reporter's work during the year, directed the work of rescuing Floyd Collins, caught in an underground chasm at Cave City, Ky., until militia arrived to take charge of the situation. Even then he slipped past the soldiers on guard and risked his life to make a last visit to the entrapped Collins.

Miller, whose everyday name is "Skeets," was born in Louisville, and went directly from high school to the police court beat of the Courier-Journal. He is now only twenty-two. As a reporter, he said frankly he had no interest in newspaper work. He wanted to be a singer, he said, and had become a reporter to get money to take him to Europe for a musical education.

He had been three years on the Courier-Journal, when he was sent one night to investigate the story that a man had been caught eighty feet underground in a sandstone cave. Miller took complete charge of the rescue of Floyd Collins the following morning. He is very small, weighs only 110 pounds, and was able to slip down the tortuous passage until he lay beside Collins. With his fingers he dug away the earth which obscured the stone holding Collin's feet. The earth was passed out handful by handful, by a chain of thirteen volunteers who crept down after Miller.

In a story to his paper a day later Miller wrote of his efforts:

"It hurts him when I press too heavy on him while working. But he grits his teeth and stands it as long as he can. He helped me a great deal in pushing to me a rock which was beyond my reach. By moving so much of it I was able to use an automobile jack which had been sawed in two to make it small enough. I wedged the jack in against the big stone holding Collins's foot and put my weight against it. Collins said I pushed it —that he could feel it —but the gravel and small rocks rolled down."

In all Miller made seven trips into the cave. He wrote:

"It is terrible inside. The cold, dirty water numbs me as soon as I start in. I have come to dread it, as have all others who have been in, but each of us tell ourselves that our suffering is as nothing compared to Collins's. His patience during long hours of agony, his constant hope when life seemed nearing an end, is enough to strengthen the heart of any one. Collins doesn't know it, but he is playing a very, very big part in his own rescue."

After the militia arrived at the cave reports were circulated that the story was a hoax. Miller was the chief witness in the investigation which followed, since he was one of the only two men who actually had seen Collins. After seventeen days the rescue party working under the direction of the militia reached Collins and found him dead.

Miller's stories during the first days of the rescue were quoted by the Associated Press and thus published from one end of the country to the other. The Courier-Journal gave him a bonus of $1,000.

After this exploit Miller returned to his paper, but continued as a reporter only a short time. At present he is living at Winter Haven, Fla., where he is in the ice cream manufacturing business with his father. He still intends to go to Europe, he says, to study singing.

4

WALTER DURANTY
After the Russian Revolution

BETWEEN 1921 AND 1934, THE FLEDGLING USSR UNDER-
went dramatic shifts. Lenin died, Stalin came to power, and Trotsky was
banished. A period of official sanction for free-market activities was followed by the collectivization of agriculture and the first, centrally determined, five-year plan.

Through all that period, the *New York Times'* Moscow correspondent
was Walter Duranty, an Englishman born in 1884. Duranty, an opinionated, eccentric reporter, won a Pulitzer Prize in 1932 for coverage that
included an eleven-part series on the Soviet Union based on his more than
a decade of observation. The articles in the series show the writing skill
and wide knowledge of both Russia and the intellectual currents of the
time that caused Duranty's work to be much admired both at the time and
by succeeding generations of Moscow correspondents.

Duranty, who was dogged by criticism that he had become an apolo-
gist for the new Communist regime, gave up his Moscow post in 1934,
after which he continued to write on a limited basis for the *Times,* and to
lecture. In a memoir written in 1935 entitled *I Write As I Please,* Duranty
acknowledged that at least some of the criticism might have been justified
—but only because he had become almost too good at his job. For a time,
Duranty wrote, he had been so caught up in trying to predict the Moscow
party line that when his expectations were confirmed, "I was so pleased
with my own judgment that I allowed my critical faculty to lapse and failed
to pay proper attention to the cost and immediate consequence of the
policies that I had foreseen."

Following is an excerpt from the first of the stories in Duranty's
prizewinning series, after which is a passage from *I Write As I Please* that
gives a flavor of Duranty's life in the Soviet Union during the early years
of Stalin's reign.

THE NEW YORK TIMES
June 14, 1931

RED RUSSIA OF TODAY RULED BY STALINISM, NOT BY COMMUNISM
by
WALTER BURANTY

Paris—Russia today cannot be judged by Western standards or interpreted in Western terms. Western Marxists and Socialists go nearly as far wrong about it as the "bourgeois" critics because they fail to understand that the dominant principle of the Soviet Union, though called Marxism or Communism, is now a very different thing from the theoretical conception advanced by Karl Marx.

In thirteen years Russia has transformed Marxism—which was only a theory anyway—to suit its racial needs and characteristics, which are strange and peculiar, and fundamentally more Asiatic than European.

The dominant principle in Russia today is not Marxism or even Leninism, although the latter is its official title, but Stalinism, to use a word which Joseph Stalin deprecates and rejects. I mean that, just as Leninism meant Marxian theory plus practical application, plus Russia, so Stalinism denotes a further development from Leninism and bears witness to the prodigious influence of the Russian character and folkways upon what seemed the rigid theory of Marx.

Stalinism is a tree that has grown from the alien seed of Marxism planted in Russian soil, and whether Western Socialists like it or not it is a Russian tree.

Old Russia was an amorphous mass, held together by a mystic, half Asian idea of an imperial regime wherein the emperor was exalted to the position of God's vice regent, with limitless power over the bodies, souls, property and even thoughts of his subjects. That, at least, was the theory, and it was only when the Czars themselves began to question it and "act human" that a spirit of doubt and eventual rebellion became manifest.

The Czarist regime was poisoned by the European veneer that was spread over Russia—a veneer that was foreign and at bottom unwelcome to the mass of the Russian people—and one of the things the Bolshevist revolution did was to sweep away this alien crust and give the essential Russianinity underneath an opportunity to breathe and grow. Which explains why the Bolsheviki, who at first were a mere handful among Russia's millions, were able successfully to impose their dominant principle—namely Marxism—which in superficial appearance was far more alien than the Germanized or Westernized system it overthrew.

The truth is that the ideas outlined in the Communist Manifesto of Marx (which incidentally expounds his whole philosophy far more simply, lucidly and concretely than the ponderous "Das Kapital" and should be learned by heart by any one who wishes to understand the Soviet Union) suited the Russian masses much better than the Western theory of individualism and private enterprise imported by Peter the Great and his successors, who finally perished in the conflict it involved with the native character of Russia.

WALTER DURANTY:
THE STORY BEHIND THE STORY

From *I Write As I Please*

The exile of Trotzky, who was sent to Alma Ata, formerly Verney, on the borders of China in south-east Kazakstan, gave rise to an extraordinary incident. I witnessed it myself in the company of Paul Sheffer, correspondent of the *Berliner Tageblatt* and am certain about the facts. One morning early in 1928 Sheffer and I learned that Trotzky with his wife and two secretaries, and I think his son, was to leave Moscow that afternoon on the Tashkent train at four o'clock or thereabouts. An hour before train time we went to the Kazan Station and found the central hall and the approaches to the Tashkent platform packed with people. . . .

About ten minutes before train time there was a stir and buzz of voices from inside the station, no shouting or actual noise, but what is described in parliamentary reports as "movement in the audience," followed by a ripple along the crowded platform as everyone craned forward eagerly to see. Down the narrow gangway hurried a little procession, two uniformed guards, then a woman and three men with porters carrying baggage and two more guards in the rear. The third man was a short erect figure wearing an astrakhan cap pulled down over his ears, a thick muffler, and a heavy fur coat—it was bitterly cold weather. He carried his head high, but looked neither to the right nor to the left, nor said a word. In a moment all four passengers had disappeared into the sleeping-car. As they had passed along the platform a low wave of sound followed them, as everyone breathed simultaneously, "*Vot* Trotzky.". . .

Two days later Sheffer came to me in great excitement. "Did you send that Trotzky story?" he asked. "Of course," I said, "didn't you?" "Naturally," he nodded, "but tell me, are you sure it was Trotzky we saw?" "Of course I'm sure," I said; "everyone else at the station saw him." "So did I," said Sheffer, "but we didn't. You and I and all the rest of them were wrong; there was no Trotzky at the Kazan Station. Trotzky and his wife were taken from their home the next day, put into an automobile and driven to Lubertzee, twenty miles from Moscow, where they entered the Tashkent train. That is the real truth—I know it from an unimpeachable source."

At first I refused to believe it, but of course he was right, and if any doubt were possible Sheffer's version is confirmed by Trotzky's own biography. So there it was—the authorities, presumably fearing that Trotzky might attempt to address the crowd and cause a disturbance, or at least an undignified scuffle, which they wished to avoid, had deliberately arranged a "Potemkin" or bogus Trotzky for the sake of public peace. I heard afterwards that the central figure was an actor who had impersonated Trotzky in one of the Civil War films. Am I not right, when people ask me how I handle news in Russia, to reply that my first rule is to believe nothing that I hear, little of what I read, and not all of what I see?

PART

II

THE FORTIES

5

HANSON W. BALDWIN
War in the Pacific

HE IS TALL AND THIN, AND HE HOLDS HIMSELF ERECT—
the very model of an Annapolis graduate and former military man. When
he speaks of institutions, he does so with respect, and when he speaks of
his employers, it is with admiration.

Hanson Baldwin, born in 1903, began working for the *New York
Times* in 1929 and became the *Times'* military correspondent in the years
leading up to World War II. It was in that capacity that he won a Pulitzer
Prize in 1943 for reports on a war tour of the Southwest Pacific that
revealed that the American forces in that area were disorganized and badly
led.

Retired now and living with his wife in the hills of western Connect-
icut, Mr. Baldwin recalls his early years in journalism with nostalgia and a
sense of humor. "There was a cartoon that ran in the *New Yorker* at the
time," he says with a laugh. "The butler coming in and saying: 'Some press
men and the gentleman from the *New York Times* are here.'" Hanson
Baldwin is, still, the gentleman from the *Times*.

Following is a portion of the first story in the series Baldwin wrote
after his Pacific tour.

THE NEW YORK TIMES
October 23, 1942

JAPAN'S HOLD ON WEST PACIFIC NOT BROKEN IN ALMOST A YEAR
by
HANSON W. BALDWIN

Japanese domination of most of the Western Pacific and much of Eastern Asia has not yet been seriously challenged in almost a year of war.

But the United States, aided by a clear-cut qualitative air superiority, has assumed the offensive. And if we can hold our Solomons foothold, we shall have taken the first small step in a campaign that may some day lead to the gates of Tokyo.

The struggle in the Pacific, as viewed by this correspondent during the course of a 14,000-mile flight over the Pacific from San Francisco to Hawaii to the Solomons and return, is a bitter, relentless "no-quarter" war that cannot be won quickly or easily. In the opinion of most of the men who are fighting this war the Japanese are more dangerous foes than the Germans, and they consider Japan, rather than Germany, the primary adversary. Others, with a broader global view of the world conflict, agree with the prevailing strategic concept that our main effort must first be directed against Hitler-dominated Europe, but emphasize that the Pacific cannot safely be considered a secondary, or minor "front.". . .

The enemy is tough and hard and relentless; as the men who are doing the fighting say, he is a "very dangerous and worthy foe." But we probably have as much to fear from our own weaknesses and our own mistakes as we do from the enemy. We can "take" the enemy and solve the gigantic problems that the Pacific campaign presents if we eliminate past and present frictions and handicaps and learn from our past mistakes. We are now trying to do in the Solomons the first small part of a major job in the Pacific.

We have done some of it well, some of it brilliantly, some of it very badly. How quickly we can do the major part of the job and at what cost depends primarily upon ourselves.

Recent operations in the Solomons—part of an oceanic campaign unprecedented in the history of war—have been costly to both sides and well illustrate the problems that confront us in the Pacific.

Perhaps our greatest problem, as it is the problem of any peace-loving nation flung suddenly into war against a nation of professional militarists, is leadership. Errors of judgment or professional mistakes on the part of some, but by no means all, of our naval leaders—errors that stem in large measure from overcaution and the defensive complex—have resulted in costly and unnecessary losses.

There still exists, too, though rarely in the front "lines," an underlying bitterness of feeling between the services, usually expressed by officers of the medium and junior grades, in criticism of the Navy by the Army air forces, and vice versa. This has been exacerbated by many of the more virulent and vocal writers and critics at home. Secretary of War Stimson wisely commented when he silenced one of the Army spokesmen that the Army was fighting the enemy, not the Navy.

HANSON BALDWIN:
THE STORY BEHIND THE STORY

My father was managing editor of the *Baltimore Sun* for a time and it was through him that I got an introduction to a retired *Times* editor, Carr Van Anda, a brilliant man who had understood Einstein's theory and played it on the front page. I got a trial job that started just three days after the stock market crash. They paid me the magnificent salary of $75 a week, subject to being reduced to $65 if I didn't make good in the first three months. I did get the cut to $65. The *Times* was a very hard paper to break into for a young man because the then-city editor who gave out the assignments never gave the new men much of a chance on a big story. The assistant city editor was an entirely different type of person. He gave me a break on a murder story and I got my $10 back.

The *Times* was a very friendly place in those days. It was small enough that you knew everybody. The star reporters sat in the row nearest the city editor and others of lesser rank fell back from there. During the Depression they never fired anybody. They gave us two pay cuts instead. There were very few bylines when I got there but in the Depression there came to be more; if you did a good story, instead of a raise, you'd get a byline. The paper was noted for its wordiness, and that came about because they paid by space until just after I came on the paper. The arrangements were made individually with each reporter as to how much he got per column.

Arthur Sulzberger, the publisher, was not the best businessman in the world; he put other things first. The paper was a national trust, he thought, a public trust, a family trust, and he felt the responsibility very strongly. Those were the days when the *Times* turned down advertisements in order to put news in the paper. They'd have little boxes on the front page that would say: "Due to the urgency of news the *Times* is forced to omit so many columns of advertising." That's changed hasn't it? It's too bad. Because that's the kind of paper you liked to work for.

I was interested in the sea and in naval matters and I worked very hard in my spare time to develop this beat. After awhile it became clear that there was going to be war in Europe and in 1937 Mr. Sulzberger told me that from now on he wanted me to do military only, and I was to pick my own assignments. It was an age when specialization was just starting in the newspaper field. There had always been specialization in drama and movies but not in the news field. So, not knowing quite what to do with me, the editors gave me a desk in a partitioned-off section where the other specialists were—sitting between the music critic and the dance critic.

I was able to find out what was going on in the military because I had friends—former classmates—who were officers. When they realized that I was going to try to report the news factually they talked rather openly, on the assumption that I wouldn't quote them as such. The GIs were generally only too glad to talk. There also wasn't the adversarial attitude between correspondents and government officials that was created in Vietnam and that exists today. The correspondents I knew put their American citizenship and winning the war first and being a correspondent second. When it comes to the state of mind of "We'll tell you what Russia says and we'll tell you what the United States says" it's bad, because you're undercutting your own country.

On my trip to the Solomon Islands I got into Guadalcanal on a Marine DC-3 crammed with gasoline drums and ammunition flown by a classmate of mine, a Marine officer. We had to dodge enemy planes along the way. What surprised me when I got there was that we held so little territory —about the equivalent of LaGuardia Field. The impression back in the States was that we had the whole island. I found out about the number of ships that had been sunk and about how badly led our forces were and how the Japanese torpedoes were deadly and ours missed their marks. I heard the people from one service cussing out the other service; there was a serious lack of coordination. At Henderson Field, the night before I arrived the Japanese had made a counterattack and gotten right in to the headquarters itself. When I got there they even had the chief cook carrying a rifle. Vice-Admiral Robert Ghormley, who was in charge of that part of the Pacific, was a planner but not a doer. There was an air of defeatism about his headquarters. He himself said, "We're doing this on a shoestring"—he used that expression. He was, but that attitude isn't the way you win wars. You've got to imbue an air of confidence.

I found the situation in the Solomons was so much different from what the American people at home thought it was that I knew I had a story and I had to get it out. I couldn't get it out down there, though, because of the censorship. Censorship was very heavy at the beginning of the war and very inept in the Pacific. A lot of failed submarine commanders were made censors. I remember once I used the term ack-ack for antiaircraft fire. It was a well-known term in World War I but the censor struck it out. I asked him why and he said, "Well, I thought you were writing in code."

So I came back to Washington and New York, wrote my stories, fought them through censorship, and was lucky enough to have a world-wide scoop when they were published. I was actually called before one of the committees of the joint chiefs of staff, made up of generals and admirals, to tell them privately what was happening in the South Pacific. The navy had kept it so quiet that the army and air force members of the committee really didn't know.

DANIEL DE LUCE:
THE STORY BEHIND THE STORY

The AP decided in 1939 that all hell was going to break loose in Europe and I was sent over as part of their plan to beef up the staff. I had had one semester of German in college five years before so their first idea was to send me to Berlin, but in the end I was sent to Budapest. Gee, I was thrilled to death, it seemed so romantic. Alma and I were there for two years. I covered the war in Poland and the war in Albania and the breakup of Iran. We had quite a few Hungarian friends, most of them Jewish. Budapest had a population of nearly a million people, and about half of them were Jewish. It was a marvelous community—some of the country's brightest musicians, actors and authors. They were dreadfully depressed because there was a Hungarian Nazi-type party that was becoming very obstreperous politically, but there was no inkling that there was going to be a holocaust. That thing didn't really get going until 1942.

During the summer of 1943 I was sort of straw-boss of the AP office in Algiers. There was a little junket arranged by the British to take some correspondents over to the British eighth army, which was then proceeding through the hind end of Tunisia.

We went over there and talked to Montgomery, who was very affable, and then we went to an airfield that had just been laid out. All of a sudden some German planes came over and dropped some small bombs and machine-gunned the airdrome. I jumped into a foxhole and an NBC correspondent jumped in on top of me. The raid was very short and when it was over we decided to get the hell out of there, so we got back in our staff car and proceeded toward the other side of the airfield.

As we neared the edge, some more German planes came over and this time there wasn't a real foxhole to get into, just sort of a depression in the ground. I put my hands behind my head to protect it and I thought, 'If I hold my breath, the thing will be over before I have to take another breath.' It went on the longest time, and all of a sudden, I felt—Bang! a solid blow, and it was hot, and I could feel the blood starting to ooze. Finally the raid was over. I was lying next to an RAF officer and I told him, 'I think I've been hit.' So he looked over and handed me a piece of hot metal. It had bruised me but it never broke the skin. But psychologically I'd gone through the whole thing of being hit.

When the Allies made the decision to invade the mainland of Italy from Sicily in September, I went with Montgomery and the Eighth Army across the Messina Strait. Two or three of the British correspondents were assigned to go with the invasion force on D-Day but the Australians and I were scheduled to go over a couple days later. So we went down to the beach on D-Day and there was a nice burly British naval officer and he was waving amphibious trucks piled high with ammunition cases and petrol tins into the water. We asked if we could sort of hitch-hike across and he said, "Oh, sure." So we got on top of the ammunition cases and the trucks went into the water and chugged over to the Italian mainland, just like that.

Montgomery was a very cautious man. I wouldn't like to use the word unfairly but he was a careful plodder and he always wanted to be absolutely sure that the odds were all in his favor. I always thought to myself that if I were a British soldier there was only one British general I'd want to serve under and that would be Montgomery because I knew he'd be careful of my life. I remember that he had a captured Italian kind of trailer that he used, nicely outfitted. He loved it. He had a canary and chintz curtains.

Montgomery moved so slowly that we correspondents actually got to Salerno a day ahead of his army. A group of nine of us went through about fifty miles of territory that was a noman's land. The Italians were very helpful. They'd telephone when we got to one town and ask "Are the Germans there?" "Oh no." One time the answer came back, "Oh yes, there's a German armored vehicle here," so we got out and hid in an orchard in case the Germans came down to scout our little town, but they didn't. When we got to Salerno, people said, "Hey, you guys, where's the Eighth Army?" They didn't get there until the next day. Our stories got through the censors but they changed them to make it look as though we and the Eighth Army got there at the same time.

The plan was for Montgomery to go up the Adriatic coast and the main allied force to come up the other side of the country. During the month of September Montgomery kept moving up the coast, every day a new dateline. But then the American fifth army was having a tough slog, so the British stopped because they didn't want to get too far in front. I was sitting around Bari, and I read in the British army publication about what was happening over in Yugoslavia. I also met some Yugoslav army officers who had fled and I talked to them, usually in broken English but they all spoke either French or German, and I spoke a very crude kind of German. It was chaos over there. Italy had occupied the coast of Yugoslavia, and when Italy quit the war and started trying to bring its forces back home, the Germans began coming down to the coast, north to south, and taking over the towns. During the period between the Italians leaving and the Germans taking over, the partisans—the underground—came in from the bush and took over the ports.

I had this idea that I wanted to go over and see what was happening. Alma and I had spent two weeks at a resort hotel in Dubrovnik in 1940, so I knew the Dalmatian people and it was familiar territory more or less. I found out where the Italian vice-admiral had his headquarters and I talked to one of his people who said that they were sending boats across to bring back their troops. I realized I'd have to get British permission because I was accredited to the British forces. I knew that the captain in charge and his staff had dinner every night at the Imperiale Hotel, where the correspondents attached to the eighth army were billeted, so one night I went over and said to him, "I'd like to go to Yugoslavia and I understand the Italians are sending over some boats. I'd like to get on one of them and see what it's like." And he said, "Oh, don't be a damn fool." But he didn't say no. So I went back and told the vice-admiral, "The British naval captain has no objection." The Italian vice-admiral assigned me to a sponge fishing boat whose captain, a Sicilian civilian named Giuseppe Virzi, was told to go to Split to evacuate the Italian forces there.

I was so lucky. If the British Middle East Command had ever been queried by somebody in Italy saying, "Look, this correspondent wants to go over to Yugoslavia," they would have said "No, not until we say so." And then if I'd gone I would have been violating military orders and you can get kicked out for that.

I was the only AP man covering the Eighth Army so I had to be sure that any news that happened would be covered while I was away. Every correspondent had a conducting officer and mine was a very nice British captain named Charles Kessler who'd been in business before the war. I told him, "Look, I've got this opportunity to go over to Yugoslavia but this weekend the correspondents are going to see the head of the Italian royal government, Marshal Pietro Badoglio. Can you cover for me?" Well, he'd never filed a story, but he was willing. So I wrote up a series of forms for him to fill in, and explained about things like how you never put more than two-hundred words in a take—a page—and you always try to repeat a little on each take so that if one gets lost the desk can make out what it was. I was gone four days altogether, and he covered for me. I gave him five pounds and he was happy and I was happy.

As it turned out, the weather was bad and we had to wait for two nights before we could go. While we were waiting, the news came that the Germans had taken Split, our original destination. So we were then told just to go across to any place on the Yugoslav coast and bring back whatever Italians were there. We left Bari early one morning and hugged the coast going sort of northwest and around a kind of peninsula. After dark, we went out to sea. The boat just sort of pooped along, doing three or maybe four knots. I didn't know enough to be scared. I was just happy that we hadn't left when we were scheduled to and gone to Split.

I dozed after awhile and when I awakened we were in a little cove; we'd come to an island off the Yugoslav coast. When we got in they'd got some branches from bushes on the shore and put them over the deck as a sort of camouflage. I looked up and there was a Yugoslav kid about fifteen or sixteen years old. I remember that he told me he had an uncle or some other relative in San Pedro, California. There was also an older partisan. The captain palavered with them and got over the point that we would like to be taken to headquarters. So we waited around until a one-cylinder automobile came down the road and took us back to the headquarters in a little village on the top of a mountain that was about five-hundred feet high. The car had at least two flat tires going a quarter of a mile so we ended up walking to the village, where we met the partisan brigade commander and the village priest.

The brigade commander had about sixty troops and they put on a military review for me out there in the square. They seemed to have the general support of the population and the priest even gave a salute. I don't know what his true feelings were but I think he was awfully glad to see Yugoslavs running a part of Yugoslavia. The partisans were very boastful about the problems they were causing the Germans and they wanted all sorts of weapons and supplies from the Allies.

They were courteous and considerate but sort of brusque. Of course Yugoslavs are kind of brusque anyway; they're a hardy Balkan people and the niceties are not their strong suit. They had red stars and so forth but they never said anything about the proletariat, or anything like that—they knew that when you're dealing with the capitalist press, so called, you don't waste your time debating ideology. They also talked about their leader, Tito, whom they idolized. Tito had organized a kind of national liberation front appealing to Yugoslavs of all political faiths, or at least that was the propaganda. I just observed and took down everything they told me. But I was disturbed by the fact that when they sang songs for us, they weren't about Eisenhower or Montgomery or Churchill, they were about the Russian marshal Timoshenko. At that time, there was this big alliance between the Soviet Union and the Western countries and everything was hunky dory. But what I saw made me wonder how the Western powers and the Soviet Union would get along after the war. I thought at the time that Tito was just a stooge of the Kremlin; I didn't know that the Yugoslavs under Tito would get fed up with Soviet domineering tactics and want to be a third force.

We stayed in the village from about ten in the morning until five or six o'clock and then we went back down to the boat. At one point a German plane came over on reconnaissance, a big two-engine bomber, and everyone hid in the brush. It turned out that there were no Italian soldiers on the island but we loaded up with some Jewish refugees and then set out. We went all night across the Adriatic and then along the coast at daylight and got back to Bari sometime that day. I hustled over to the Imperiale Hotel, got out my typewriter, and started writing.

I worked as late as possible that night and I finished about noon the next day. I wrote the story in five dispatches, splitting it up by topics. I was leery about the censorship so I dealt with the political situation in the fifth dispatch, raising the question of whether the Western powers were going to be able to work with Tito after the war, when as far as I could see the Tito forces were obviously going to be the dominant force. I saw it as a test of relations between the Soviet Union and the Western powers. A Canadian public relations officer came up to my hotel room and I had the five pieces all done by that time so he took them out to the airport to put them in the pouch to send them to Algiers for censorship. He told me afterward that he opened them up on the way to the airport and read them and decided, "De Luce has got a good story."

Ed Kennedy, the AP chief of bureau in Algiers, dumped them all in the censors' office and then he kept checking and asking how they were coming along. One after another of the first four was finally passed with some deletions but they said they were sending the fifth one on to Cairo, which was the headquarters of the Middle East Command. That's where they had the high political brains and if they had a question, they asked Winston about it. That dispatch never saw the light of day.

Sometimes the military censorship was an effort to cover up snafus and sometimes you had to question the correctness of the logic and how it was being applied. But I was inclined to give the command the benefit of the doubt. If our side messed up it wasn't a story for me. You felt yourself a part of the effort and you felt that if you weren't actually a combat participant at least you didn't want to do anything that would mess things up for the people who had to do the fighting.

There was a news conference with Montgomery the tail end of the week after my stories started appearing in the United States and in England, too. All the other guys — by then there were ten or twelve correspondents covering the Eighth Army—came over and shook my hand and said, "Nice going." It was nice of them to be congratulatory, because in those days you could get what they called a "blivet"—sounds like "rivet" and is meant to convey a similar impression, a red-hot hunk of discomfort to the unfortunate wretch out in the field. You know, "De Luce says. . .where's yours?" As it turned out, my stories ran in October of 1943 and it wasn't until May of 1944 that two correspondents accredited to the British Middle East Command were allowed to go into Yugoslavia. So for all that time my stories with the Yugoslav datelines stood alone. How lucky can you get? It was a once in a lifetime thing.

7

HOMER BIGART
Hiroshima After the Bomb

TO READ HOMER BIGART'S WAR DISPATCHES IS TO BE TRANS-
ported back to some of the grittiest battlefields of the twentieth century.
In conversational, straightforward prose, Bigart, who was born in 1907,
brought the sounds and smells of war to the readers of the *New York
Herald Tribune* and later, the *New York Times*: the storming of Iwo Jima
in World War II, MacArthur's ill-planned offensive in Korea, America's
treacherous slide into Vietnam. In the process, he won two Pulitzer Prizes,
one in 1946 for his coverage of the Pacific in World War II, and the other
in 1951, shared with five other Korean War correspondents.

Today, white-haired and ruddy-faced, Bigart lives with his wife in an
old farmhouse in New Hampshire. He is still recognizable from an affec-
tionate description in *Editor & Publisher* in 1949 commenting on how his
appearance clashed with the image conjured up by his exploits. In fact,
said *E & P,* rather than looking like the dashing young hero of an adven-
ture tale, Bigart was middle-aged and "somewhat on the plump side."

Bigart's final battle dispatch of World War II, dated August 15, 1945,
was datelined "In a B-29 over Japan" and began: "The radio tells us that
the war is over, but from where I sit it looks suspiciously like a rumor. A
few minutes ago—at 1:32 A.M.—we fire-bombed Kamagaya, a small industrial city behind Tokyo near the northern edge of Kanto Plain. Peace
was not official for the Japanese either, for they shot right back at us." The
dispatch ended with the scene inside the bomber on the way back to base.
"Everyone relaxed. We tried to pick up San Francisco on the radio but
couldn't. The gunners took out photos of their wives and girl friends and
said: 'Hope this is the last, baby.'"

And it was. As Bigart explained in a postscript, they returned to
Guam to find that they had just been on the last raid of the war.

What set Bigart's dispatches apart was not only the intensely vivid sense of being there that they conveyed, but also the clear voice that came through: Bigart was a kind of Everyman, taking in events around him and reporting them without affectation. In his story on the last raid, Bigart described the reaction inside the bomber's cabin when the radio picked up a San Francisco station and heard an announcer reporting that people were celebrating the end of the war. " 'Yeah,' said one of the crewmen disgustedly," Bigart wrote, 'they're screaming and we're flying.' "

Through it all, Bigart maintained his sense of humor and an unwillingness to take himself too seriously. He didn't like competing with fellow *Tribune* correspondent Marguerite Higgins in Korea, he says, because she was too keen. "When I came out I thought I was the premier war correspondent and I thought that she, being the Tokyo correspondent, ought to be back in Tokyo," he says with a chuckle. "But she didn't see things that way. She was a very brave person, foolishly brave. As a result, I felt as though I had to go out and get shot at occasionally myself. So I resented that."

That sense of humor, accompanied by plain hard work, won Bigart the admiration of his fellow journalists. One, who knew Bigart in Korea, later told *Newsweek* that "The idea of being best by out-smarting the competition never occurred to Homer. He'd just go ahead and do his work, and when it came to writing the story, nine times out of ten you could count on his being the best."

Bigart was a witness to many historical events, including being one of the first correspondents to visit Hiroshima after the dropping of the atom bomb. That dispatch, a portion of which follows, formed part of the entry for which he was awarded the 1946 Pulitzer Prize.

NEW YORK HERALD TRIBUNE
September 5, 1945

A MONTH AFTER THE ATOM BOMB: HIROSHIMA STILL CAN'T BELIEVE IT
by
HOMER BIGART

HIROSHIMA, Japan, Sept. 3 (Delayed)—We walked today through Hiroshima, where survivors of the first atomic-bomb explosion four weeks ago are still dying at the rate of about one hundred daily from burns and infections which the Japanese doctors seem unable to cure.

The toll from the most terrible weapon ever devised now stands at 53,000 counted dead, 30,000 missing and presumed dead, 13,960 severely wounded and likely to die, and 43,000 wounded. The figures come from Hirokuni Dadai, who, as "chief of thought control" of Hiroshima Prefecture, is supposed to police subversive thinking.

On the morning of Aug. 6 the 340,000 inhabitants of Hiroshima were awakened by the familiar howl of air-raid sirens. The city had never been bombed—it had little industrial importance. The Kure naval base lay only twelve miles to the southeast and American bombers had often gone there to blast the remnants of the imperial navy, or had flown mine-laying or strafing missions over Shimonoseki Strait to the west. Almost daily enemy planes had flown over Hiroshima, but so far the city had been spared.

At 8 a.m. the "all clear" sounded. Crowds emerged from the shallow raid shelters in Military Park and hurried to their jobs in the score of tall, modern, earthquake-proof buildings along the broad Hattchobori, the main business street of the city. Breakfast fires still smoldered in thousands of tiny ovens—presently they were to help to kindle a conflagration.

Very few persons saw the Superfortress when it first appeared more than five miles above the city. Some thought they saw a black object swinging down on a parachute from the plane, but for the most part Hiroshima never knew what hit it.

A Japanese naval officer, Vice-Admiral Masao Kanazawa, at the Kure base said the concussion from the blast twelve miles away was "like the great wind that made the trees sway." His aide, a senior lieutenant who was to accompany us into the city, volunteered that the flash was so bright even in Kure that he was awakened from his sleep. So loud was the explosion that many thought the bomb had landed within Kure.

When Lieutenant Taira Ake, a naval surgeon, reached the city at 2:30 p.m. he found hundreds of wounded still dying unattended in the wrecks and fields on the northern edge of the city. "They didn't look like human beings," he said. "The flesh was burned from their faces and hands, and many were blinded and deaf. . . ."

In the part of the town east of the river the destruction had looked no different from a typical bomb-torn city in Europe. Many buildings were only partly demolished, and the streets were still choked with debris.

But across the river there was only flat, appalling desolation, the starkness accentuated by bare, blackened tree trunks and the occasional shell of a reinforced concrete building.

We drove to Military Park and made a walking tour of the ruins.

By all accounts the bomb seemed to have exploded directly over Military Park. We saw no crater there. Apparently the full force of the explosion was expended laterally.

Aerial photographs had shown no evidence of rubble, leading to the belief that everything in the immediate area of impact had been literally pulverized into dust. But on the ground we saw this was not true. There was rubble everywhere, but much smaller in size than normal.

Approaching the Hattchobori, we passed what had been a block of small shops. We could tell that only because of office safes that lay at regular intervals on sites that retained little else except small bits of iron and tin. Sometimes the safes were blown in.

The steel door of a huge vault in the four-story Geibi Bank was flung open, and the management had installed a temporary padlocked door. All three banking houses—Geibi, Mitsubishi and the Bank of Japan—were conducting business in the sturdy concrete building of the Bank of Japan, which was less damaged than the rest.

We stood uneasily at the corner of the bank building, feeling very much like a youth walking down Main Street in his first long pants. There weren't many people abroad—a thin trickle of shabbily dressed men and women—but all of them stared at us. There was hatred in some glances, but generally more curiosity than hatred. We were representatives of an enemy power that had employed a weapon far more terrible and deadly than poison gas, yet in the four hours we spent in Hiroshima none so much as spat at us, nor threw a stone. . . .

Neither Dadai nor local correspondents who asked for an interview seemed to believe that the atomic bomb would end war. One of the first questions asked by Japanese newspaper men was: "What effect will the bomb have on future wars?" They also asked whether Hiroshima "would be dangerous for seventy years." We told them we didn't know.

HOMER BIGART:
THE STORY BEHIND THE STORY

I was brought up in the '20s when all kids thought like they do in the present generation that they didn't have to really work; they were going to get richer and richer. It's incredible but we thought we didn't have to do anything. I decided I would become an architect because it sounded so prestigious and so easy. Especially easy. We lived in Hawley, in northeastern Pennsylvania, where my father, who'd started as a millhand, owned his own textile mill. I went to what was then Carnegie Tech in Pittsburgh and quickly discovered that if you were going to be an architect you at least had to learn how to draw. But I couldn't even do that. The only passing grade I got was English so I decided that about the only thing I could do was to become a newspaperman. Luckily a high school pal of mine had a copy boy's job on the *New York Herald Tribune* and he got me a job.

I went to New York in 1927. After awhile I started doing obits that people would phone in. The paper paid space rates then —you got paid according to how much you wrote. As a result, I wrote up many a humble person way beyond his worth. Eventually I got to doing other stories, mostly feature stuff, and for awhile I covered education. I was pretty timid so it was awfully hard for me to cover politics, because I could never ask the necessarily rude questions.

Then the war came and everything changed. I tell you, I'll never run down war. I got sent to London and those first few months were about the happiest ones I think I've ever spent in journalism. I liked the people and I liked the city. There was sort of a lull in the air raid war so you had all the excitement of being in a war area without any real danger.

But then the Air Force got this crazy idea of letting correspondents go on every major raid over Germany. At the time, February 1943, the bombers flew in daylight and without fighter escort. Casualties were heavy. The deepest penetration of Germany by American bombers was scheduled for February 26 and the target was Bremen. Six reporters went along. We never saw Bremen. Too many clouds. So we flew around and bombed the secondary target, Wilhelmshaven. Or thought we did. What we did see quite plainly was a rising swarm of German fighters. They got seven of our sixty bombers including the one with the *New York Times* correspondent. That put a long halt to taking newsmen on raids. It was bad publicity.

After six months in London I was sent down to North Africa and I covered the invasion of Sicily and Italy from there. I never deliberately got into the thick of the fighting but I found being at headquarters such a rotten bore and the army personnel so awful that I just wanted to get away. The job of the officers at headquarters was to give out propaganda but the ones in the field, the actual field commanders, would tell the truth.

I didn't want to leave Europe for the Pacific but the paper asked me to go so I did. I was in Okinawa when the bomb was dropped on Hiroshima. An Air Force general showed me air photographs of Hiroshima but I wasn't terribly impressed. I got to see it for myself a month later when they organized a trip for about a dozen correspondents. I don't know what I was expecting but it was visually an enormous letdown. None of us knew what Hiroshima had looked like before the bomb but I think we were expecting to see vast heaps of debris as in Hamburg or Dresden or Coventry or London. But apparently the bomb demolished everything. There were only a few shells of buildings left standing, those made of iron and steel. And of course most of Hiroshima had been made of wood and it was just consumed by fire.

We traveled around a few blocks on foot in the center of the city but there really wasn't much to see. There were no civilians to talk to because everyone had been ordered out. Some Japanese officers kept warning us not to loiter but we were suspicious of their warnings. In fact they were doing the correct thing because if we had hung around very long we probably wouldn't be here today. I knew nothing about radiation at the time and I don't think most of the Americans knew any more, although certainly the army knew enough by then not to send troops in.

It's very easy to look back and express shock and horror but the fact is that at the time we thought it was just a hell of a good raid, just another big bomb. We were still full of the war spirit and Japan was an all-out war. We felt we had to win it and that we had to practically exterminate the enemy. Hatred was something you lived with. I'm very suspicious of people's expressions of shock now. They've forgotten how they felt then.

After the war I was in Poland and then in Yugoslavia. While I was there, the Greek Communist emigres approached me in my hotel room and asked me if I would like to go to see their leader, General Markos. I said yes immediately although the NBC correspondent, George Polk, had been slain in Salonica while he was said to have been on his way to see him.

The Greeks made an appointment to meet me at night on a street corner. They took me down to the railroad yards and put me into a blacked-out coach that was later hitched onto a train going to the capital of Macedonia. When we got there I was kept in this compartment until all the other passengers had left. Then I was taken out and put in a truck with the canvas down and given a tire to sit on. The road from there to the border of Greece was pretty rough and we were several hours on the road. I was mystified by all the secrecy when we got down to the border because I didn't know at that time that Tito had broken with Moscow. The result of that was that Markos and the Greek Communists didn't know where they stood in relationship to Yugoslavia. From the truck we switched to horses and mules and after two days of riding on a trail we got to Markos' camp.

In fact the interview was a disappointment because we couldn't find an interpreter that was any good and because it was all propaganda. But what made it a story was the getting there. Afterward, I got across the Greek lines into royalist territory and went down to Athens. The Greek Prime Minister called me in and questioned me about the route I had taken. I told him and he said, "That can't be right, because our troops hold the surrounding area." And I said, "Not all the time."

But then, after I'd written my story and sent it to New York, thinking that this was a real feat, nothing appeared. It wasn't until later that I heard part of the story. It seems there was a difference of opinion among the top brass. Some thought it too leftist. Remember, the Red Scare was on. Westbrook Pegler was calling the *Trib* the "Uptown Daily Worker." McCarthy hadn't become terribly well known then but Pegler was leading the cry. The story was held for a week until the chief editorial writer told the owners that they just had to run it, and they did, but I understand that some remarks of mine that were thought to be "Commie" were extracted from it. I've never seen how it appeared because I was too pissed-off to read it.

World War II is the only war I felt that we had to be in. Korea was not a victory and Vietnam was a defeat. It's amazing that so few years after the World War a string of presidents—Kennedy, Johnson, Nixon—could so easily get us entangled on the continent of Asia. And it'll happen again. I don't think we've learned anything.

PART
III

THE FIFTIES

□

8

EDWIN O. GUTHMAN

"Un-American Activities" in Seattle

THE IMAGE OF JOSEPH MCCARTHY STILL CASTS A LONG shadow over Americans' memories of the 1950s. Hardly had the sounds of World War II abated before the Soviet Union, an ally during the latter part of the war, was firmly established as an evil giant bent on global domination. And with that perception came the rise of what came to be known as McCarthyism, the practice of publicly naming purported Communists and hounding them from their jobs.

What is sometimes not appreciated is that Senator McCarthy was by no means the first to engage in Red-baiting on a grand scale. In 1947, the Washington State legislature set up its own Un-American Activities Committee, known as the Canwell committee.

One of the places that was hardest hit was the University of Washington in Seattle, where in 1948 more than a half-dozen faculty members were accused of Communist party membership. The most celebrated case was that of philosophy professor Melvin Rader, who, it was claimed, had attended a secret Communist training school in New York State during the summer of 1938.

In a book entitled *False Witness* that he later wrote about his experiences, Rader recalled the anxiety he felt when first faced with the prospect of possible dismissal from his teaching post—a fate that eventually befell three of his colleagues. At the time, he had a wife and four young children to support. "If their strategy was to make me 'break,' they were close to succeeding," he wrote.

Rader's concerns for himself and his family were well-placed: in the months after the accusations against him were made, his career went into professional limbo and his family experienced incidents of harassment. Ultimately, however, he found a champion in the *Seattle Times,* which conducted an independent investigation into the charges and concluded that Rader was innocent. Based on the paper's evidence, and that collected by Rader himself, the University president announced that Rader was absolved of any suspicion of guilt. Edwin Guthman, the reporter responsible for the newspaper investigation, won a Pulitzer Prize in 1950 for his work.

Guthman stayed with the *Seattle Times* until 1961, with a year out as a Nieman fellow at Harvard. Later, after working for Robert Kennedy, he became a top editor at the *Los Angeles Times* and the *Philadelphia Inquirer*. Now retired and living in California, Guthman, who was born in 1919, says that what prompted the *Seattle Times'* efforts—in Rader's behalf and later in behalf of others swept up in the maelstrom—was a concern for due process and fair play. "They were old-fashioned, real conservatives and it was simple to them," he says of his editor and the newspaper's publisher. "This was not the way you treat people." And, he suggests, if more papers had followed their example, the worst excesses of the McCarthy period might never have occurred.

Following is an excerpt from a story Guthman wrote to accompany his documented chronology, which ran the day after Professor Rader had been cleared.

THE SEATTLE DAILY TIMES
October 21, 1949

RED STIGMA BIG BURDEN FOR RADER FAMILY

For Melvin Rader, slim, serious University of Washington philosophy professor, today marked the end of a long, strenuous fight to clear his name, which had been linked closely with communism.

Although Rader denied having been a Communist, and denied that he attended a secret Communist school in New York in 1938, the effect of having been accused publicly of Communist activity hit deeply into his everyday life and that of his wife and four children.

It reached into the store where the Raders bought their groceries; into the school his children attended; into his classes at the University, and into the neighborhood where he lived at 6224 23rd Av. N.W. . . . .

For Mrs. Rader and the children, Miriam, now 12 years old; Barbara, 10; Carey, 8, and David, 6, the charge struck with terror and pain. They had had no idea Rader would be involved at the legislative committee's hearing.

Rader also was unprepared. Always a liberal, Rader at various times participated vigorously in a number of organizations, such as the now defunct Washington Commonwealth Federation, which later were found to have been Communist-influenced or Communist-controlled.

Because of this, the Canwell committee suspected that Rader might have been a Communist. But, after he was interviewed twice by committee investigators before the hearing began, committee members let it be known that they did not believe Rader was a Communist.

The committee believed, however, that Rader could give considerable information about Communist activity on the campus but had not done so. It was decided to subpoena Rader and force him to sit through the hearing in the hope that he would "break."

Midway through the proceedings, [George] Hewitt told the committee that he recognized Rader as a man he had seen at the New York school. That set the stage. . . .

For the most part the Rader children were not chided or embarrassed by their playmates. In school, however, a few unpleasant incidents occurred.

Once, while Miriam's class was discussing Russia and the United States, a girl stood up and said that people could be Communists and nobody know about it.

Turning toward Miriam, the girl continued:

"In fact, the daughter of one such person is in school, I think."

That was the nearest any of the family came to receiving an open slur. Some people, who knew the Raders, were amused by Hewitt's accusation.

Shortly after the hearing, as Rader paid a bill in their neighborhood grocery store, the clerk joked:

"I have to be sure to collect the sales tax to pay Canwell."

"Yes," replied Rader, "and I have to pay to be persecuted."

EDWIN GUTHMAN:
THE STORY BEHIND THE STORY

Seattle was in one sense kind of stagnant as far as growth and progress between the two wars but the city and western Washington had a very radical political history. The first general strike in America occurred in Seattle in 1919. I remember my mother and father discussing it years afterward and what they talked about was the quietness of the city. Everything shut down, everything. My father, who was the sales manager of a wholesale grocery company, walked to work because we didn't have a car in those days. There were Communists in the shipyards and they were the nucleus of the general strike. The I.W.W. was very active there and by the '30s the Communists were involved in a number of unions.

While I was a student at the University of Washington in the late '30s, I worked nights on the *Seattle Star*. I was a member of the Newspaper Guild, and I can remember going to meetings during that period that lasted until three or four o'clock in the morning. The membership was pretty evenly split between Communists and non-Communists and the two groups sat on opposite sides of the room. You had to stay until the end because the split was so even that if people from one side left, the other side would pass resolutions that the first side opposed. The resolutions were about international things like whether the United States should give further aid to England. People would argue and argue and all the major figures in Seattle journalism would be there. The University of Washington was a place of great ferment, too, and it was a lot of fun.

Did I ever think of joining the Communist party? Hell no. There wasn't any stigma to being a Communist but I just wasn't interested in, I don't know, the rigmarole of the Communist party or any other organization, left or right. I was interested in politics but not in joining organizations; that just wasn't my way of doing business.

I went in the Army in the summer of 1941, as soon as my class graduated, and I came home on Thanksgiving Day 1945. The law was that if you had a job when you went in, you had it when you came out, so I had a job on the *Star* waiting for me. When I came back the atmosphere was quite different with regard to the Communists than it had been before. The tide was beginning to shift. In the Guild, the Communists were outnumbered and after about six months they could see they weren't going to get anywhere and they stopped coming. The whole country was changing.

During the war, the man who'd hired me had become editor of the paper, and over the next few years he gave me a basic training in journalism: I covered cops, I covered city hall, I covered the courthouse. In the summer of 1947 my wife and I were married and three weeks later, the paper folded. Fortunately I got a job on another paper, the *Seattle Times*.

I had covered the legislature that year for the first time and that was when they established a joint committee on un-American activities. I don't think there was any great pressure or public demand to have a committee. The main promoters were two newspapermen, Ashley Holden, the political writer of the Spokane *Spokesman-Review,* and Fred Niendorff, the political writer of Hearst's Seattle *Post-Intelligencer.* They both had a lot of influence, particularly Holden, and they did a lot of drum-beating. That year the Republicans took control of the state legislature for the first time since 1932 and they created the committee. Holden in fact may well have been the person who picked Albert Canwell, who was a state representative from Spokane, to head it. There wasn't any real controversy over the formation of the committee; there may have been some protests but there was no big deal.

From then on, there was no ongoing oversight of the committee because the legislature only met once every two years, for sixty days. So after this committee was created the legislature would not convene again until 1949. It had a staff of investigators and it certainly had help from the immigration department and very likely from other federal departments. They would do an investigation and then subpoena witnesses and they also had a number of witnesses who were former Communists and who were on the circuit at that time, testifying before Congress and other places.

I was assigned to cover the hearings and I thought at the beginning that the committee would do a decent job. I haven't got a lot of sympathy for people who let somebody else tell them what to think, and particularly a foreign country, and that's what people in the Communist party did. As

I watched the way the committee conducted itself, though, I became concerned about the way they were doing things—I thought they were heavy-handed.

But my job was not to make judgments; my job was to find out what was going on and report it. Of course being a reporter means seeking out the truth but I think reporters are not cops and they're not lawyers and they're not politicians. If you start getting involved on one side or another covering something like this you've lost your effectiveness. And look, I was a reporter for a relatively small newspaper in Seattle, Washington, and this was 1948. You talk about Ed Murrow and his expose of McCarthy; I mean, Ed Murrow wasn't paying tiddly squat attention at that time to what was going on. When he and the others got around to exposing what McCarthy was doing it was already into the '50s.

I had good relationships with the committee chairman and with the chief counsel, who was a man by the name of William Houston. He was becoming increasingly upset with Niendorff and Holden because they wanted to tell him how to do his job. And they wanted everything done in the afternoon since they were both morning papers and that way it would be too late for it to get into the *Times,* their competition. As a reaction to that, Houston gave me lots of stuff so that I could beat them, and I got a lot of stories.

The committee began by investigating a number of unions and then they started looking into the university. The committee was already front page news but this really attracted attention. There aren't a lot of private universities in the Pacific Northwest; the main institutions of higher learning are the state universities. People took a great deal of pride in, and interest in, the University of Washington. A great many people in the legislature and outside it were alumni.

Before the hearings began, Russell McGrath, the managing editor, asked me to find out which university professors were going to be named. And so several days before the hearings began I went over to the committee headquarters and I saw Al Canwell. He was reluctant but finally he told me the names and the eight or nine people were all familiar to me. Then I asked him about some others, among them Mel Rader. He told me that they thought Rader had been a member of the Communist party but they didn't have anybody who could identify him. He said they were going to subpoena him and have him there and see what happened.

There was a lot of tension and excitement when the hearing finally took place. People who were going to be named or their sympathizers tried to disrupt the hearings and they would be escorted out by state patrolmen. There was great resistance on the part of the people identified as Communists to being questioned and there were stirring speeches made.

One morning, they had a witness by the name of George Hewitt, a black man from New York who had been a member of the Communist party and was a witness for the Immigration Service in a number of its proceedings. I identified him as a Negro in my stories because the custom of identifying people that way was just something that was done. I don't defend it. There was certainly no sense that because Hewitt was black that made his testimony less credible or more credible than anyone else's.

Hewitt didn't have intimate knowledge of the situation in Washington State; he was one of those witnesses who testified in a broader sense about the Communist party and its involvement in political and social activities and control of the party by the Soviet Union and all that type of thing. During the course of the hearings, without much warning, he testified that he had seen Melvin Rader at a secret Communist training school in New York State in the summer of 1938. Later, he explained that he had seen Rader in the audience and made the connection. At the noon hour, after his testimony was finished, the committee took Hewitt to the airport and got him out of town. Why that was done was never quite clear. In the afternoon, Rader took the witness stand and testified that he had never been a member of the Communist party. He was very forthcoming about his activities and he didn't take the Fifth Amendment. So this question then became the cause celêbre of all the hearings, it was *the* issue: was Melvin Rader a member of the Communist party?

The committee said that it would settle the matter but months went by without anything happening. In the meantime the prosecuting attorney in Seattle charged Hewitt with perjury in the naming of Melvin Rader. In early 1949 there was an extradition hearing in New York City. The judge there refused to send Hewitt back to Seattle to stand trial, and he said the reason was that he would be sending Hewitt to his slaughter because the courts there were controlled by the Communist party.

A couple of days later when I came to work Mr. McGrath motioned to me to come into his office. Mr. McGrath had been a part of the Chicago newspaper scene of the *Front Page* era but he had decided to move West to raise his family. He had the appearance and the demeanor of a Jesuit priest, a very laconic man of great integrity and great courage. The publisher of the paper was a man named Elmer Todd, who had been the lawyer of the family that owned the paper. He had been Theodore Roosevelt's U.S. Attorney in Seattle, and he was a Roosevelt-type Republican. While his editorial policy was very conservative, his news coverage was absolutely, rigorously separate. Mr. McGrath said that it appeared that the courts were not going to settle the question about Professor Rader and that the committee was not going to, and that it was time for a newspaper to find out what had happened. And he wanted me to do that.

So that's how I spent the next couple of months. Rader had said in his testimony that in the summer of 1938 he had been with his family at Canyon Creek Lodge about forty miles northeast of Seattle. Well, if somebody says they were at a lodge at a particular time, it doesn't take a lot of brains to figure out that you should go to the lodge and ask the people if they have a register and find out what it shows. As it turned out, Canyon Creek Lodge had burned down but the woman who owned it, a Mrs. Mueller, was still there. When I told her I wanted to see the pages of her register for the summer of 1938, she said, "Oh, the Canwell Committee was here last September and they took the pages."

Well, if the pages had shown that Rader was not there, the committee would have made them public immediately, right? You didn't have to be too courageous or too smart to figure out that something was wrong.

So, then I went to Rader and asked him whether he had any other recollections of things he'd done that would enable us to substantiate where he had been. And he said yes, he had broken his glasses and had gone to an optometrist or an oculist and that he had gone to the University National Bank where he kept his bank account and had signed for his bank statement. He also remembered taking some books out of the university library, and there were a couple of other things. He had already started doing some investigating himself and so in some cases I was able to follow his leads. Some of it was easy, like going to the bank. I could examine his signature and it was something that couldn't have been forged. And the medical people had kept records, too.

But some things were more difficult. You have to remember that this had all happened ten years before. One of the things I particularly remember is spending days in the University of Washington library. Rader couldn't remember exactly what books he'd taken out but he had some idea. The library gave me access to the stacks and I spent days methodically flipping through books to see if the cards had his name and the date on them. I went through a lot of books. And I found them.

Finally, I was convinced that it would have been impossible for Rader to have been in New York and then gone to Seattle and back to New York during the period in 1938 that he was supposed to have been at the Communist training school. I went to Mr. McGrath with the evidence and he didn't have me write a thing. He told me to check out the summer of 1937 and the summer of 1939 just in case Hewitt had the year wrong. And I did the same thing: I went to Rader and said, "Okay, how can we substantiate it?" It was clear that he couldn't have gone to New York in '39 or '37 either.

At that point, Mr. McGrath took all the material into Mr. Todd and Mr. Todd's reaction to this was to call Canwell, who was in Spokane, and say, "We've got this evidence, we want you to come over here and say whatever you have to say about it. I'll give you a week, and if you don't come we're going to take this material to the president of the University of Washington and ask him to clear Professor Rader." Canwell did not come. So then I took the material out to the president of the university and went over it with him. And he did the same thing that Mr. Todd had done: he called Canwell and explained that he had strong evidence indicating that Rader was innocent of the charge and said he would give Canwell a week to come over and that if he didn't come, he would clear Rader.

So during that week I wrote the story. I worked day and night. Canwell did not come, and the president held a press conference and cleared Rader of the charges, and my story ran. People find it unusual that the paper hadn't printed a word up to that point, but again I have to go back to the two men who were responsible. This was, as they saw it, the way to do things.

At that point, of course, the missing pages of the register became a focal point of interest. Canwell was interviewed in Spokane and one of the things he said that I remember was, "If the *Seattle Times* thinks it can find the pages of the register, let them try." So the next morning, after my story ran, I came to work and of course I was elated. My story was all over the paper, and Rader had been cleared. But I didn't get by McGrath's office. He knocked on the glass as I was walking by and motioned for me to come in and he said, "You find that register."

Well, by this time the 1949 legislature had met and the Democrats had regained control and they had eliminated the Un-American Activities

Committee. The files supposedly had been put in a safe deposit vault in a bank in Olympia and the keys had been given to the speaker of the House and the president of the Senate. I assumed that the register was in there. In the late summer, the safe deposit vault was opened and there was nothing there. Nothing. Zero. There were no files, just empty boxes. The committee had never turned over its files.

That's when I went to Bill Houston, the chief counsel to the committee who had been friendly to me earlier. He was living on a farm in Oregon and I went down to see him. We talked, and finally he gave me the register. I think he did it because he was a decent guy and I think he was sick about what had happened and about the way he had been run over roughshod by Niendorff and Holden and this was his way of getting even.

You would think that this would have been the end of Canwell, but not quite. Canwell still had a lot of supporters and when Washington was given another seat in Congress as a result of the 1950 census Canwell won the Republican primary for the seat. One day a printer at the paper came to my desk and said, "Look at this." And it was an editorial for the next day supporting Canwell in the election. I took the editorial and walked over to Mr. McGrath and put it down on his desk and I said, "Did you know about this?" And he read it and he said, "No, I didn't." And he got up and walked in to see Mr. Todd. The editorial never ran. The Democrat, Don Magnuson, won, and he won by the strength of his support in Seattle. So I think that had the *Seattle Times* supported Canwell, quite likely Canwell would have been in the United States Congress.

I've always felt that if there had been a few more publishers like Elmer Todd and a few more editors like Russell McGrath the McCarthy era might have been different. The fact that Elmer Todd did what he did changed how one city, Seattle, dealt with that problem. Canwell could say, as he did say in the Washington House of Representatives, that "Ed Guthman is taking the *Seattle Times* for a ride in a little Red Wagon," but everybody knew that Elmer Todd was not going to be taken for a ride in a little red wagon by anybody. He was a leading citizen, an older man, with an impeccable record.

And it wasn't just the Rader case. When the loyalty program got going, and government employees were losing their jobs, Elmer Todd and Russell McGrath sent me and other reporters out with instructions, "You find out about this person and you get this man's job back." When the U.S.

House Un-American Activities hearings were held in 1954 in Seattle, the leading members of the Communist party were defended gratis by the officers of the Seattle Bar Association. That was the kind of practical impact Todd had. Yes, I was the one who did the work and won the prize but Elmer Todd and Russell McGrath were the ones who charted the course and set the sails and took the heat.

There's a long trail out of this Canwell thing. I was never absolutely sure that Mel Rader hadn't been a member of the Communist party, simply because of what I had seen as a college student and his activities and so forth, so whenever people came out of the Communist party I'd ask them and they all said the same thing: we tried to recruit him but he never joined. In 1954 the U.S. House Un-American Activities Committee came to Seattle and held hearings and the key witness was Barbara Hartle, one of the top Communists in the state. She had been arrested and sent to prison under the Smith Act and then had decided to become an informant. During the hearings I was able to interview her alone and I asked her, "Was Mel Rader a member of the Communist party?" And she said, "No, he was not." At that point I was convinced.

Now, I've got to bring in another person, John Goldmark, who was a student at Harvard in the 1930s, very bright, who settled in Washington State, bought a ranch there, and eventually got into politics and was elected to the state legislature. At the time he ran for reelection in 1960 the John Birch Society started attacking him on the basis that his wife had been a member of the party in the late 1930s. It was true, she had been, but she'd drifted out of it. The attack was carried on by none other than Ashley Holden, the political writer who'd pushed for the Canwell committee to be formed. He was now a member of the John Birch society and he and his son were putting out a weekly paper in the area where Goldmark lived. And Albert Canwell got into it too. Goldmark was defeated, and afterward he sued for libel.

One of the witnesses at the trial was Barbara Hartle, and among other things, she testified that Melvin Rader was a member of the Communist party. Rader had been brought into the case because Goldmark had been attacked for being a member of the American Civil Liberties Union, and the ACLU's role as a Communist front was established by the fact that Rader was an ACLU official. I was working in Washington by that time and I read about the trial in the paper. I called up John Goldmark's lawyer and I told him the story about what Barbara Hartle had told me

Americans, in particular, and Western-oriented people in general would be quick to note that there is a spiritual difference between working under the ever-present muzzle of a tommygun in the hands of an M.V.D. guard and free labor; between going home at night to a barb-wire-encircled camp and to your own room.

Having seen the free workers and the slave workers, having seen them doing identical tasks, except for the presence of the guards; having seen the barracks in which the free labor for the most part lives, this correspondent has considerable doubts as to the existence of any great spiritual differences. In fact, the conditions of life are such as to leave very little room for things of the spirit, regardless of the technical status of the individual. . . .

In the whole city of Khabarovsk, out of forty or fifty building projects *not one* was being carried out by ordinary free, civilian labor.

This correspondent stood for a while in Lenin Square, across the street from a fine-looking hospital to which a large addition was being constructed. The annex was being built, of course, by prison laborers, most of whom appeared to be women. There were M.V.D. tommygunners right beside the sidewalk at an entrance to the construction site for trucks, and hundreds of people, men and women, were strolling past.

The citizens of Khabarovsk streamed steadily past the building site. No one averted his eyes. No one looked away. In ten minutes of watching I saw no sign of interest, no sign of curiosity in the faces of the passersby.

HARRISON SALISBURY:
THE STORY BEHIND THE STORY

My first trip to Russia was as a United Press correspondent in 1944. I was in the Middle East and the editors said, "Get to Russia as fast as you can and relieve Henry Shapiro so he can take a vacation. You'll be gone a few weeks." I was terribly excited. This was before D-day and it was *the* big story of the war. The Russians were now defeating the Germans: every week advancing, recovering territory, driving the Germans back in these massive retreats, and we knew this was going to bring the war to an end.

The biggest problem I had was getting in. You couldn't fly directly into Russia so you either had to go to Iran and fly up from Tehran or go in by sea from England to Murmansk in the north. I went in through Iran and it took me about a month, because I had to wait in Tehran for a flight.

All the foreign correspondents—about fifteen or sixteen Americans, five or six Britishers and a few assorted others—lived in the Hotel Metropole right in the heart of Moscow. It was a great big old hotel that had been built in the late 1890s. It had several positive attributes: it was warm, well-heated—and most things in Moscow were not and this was winter-time—and it had a consistent food supply. Almost everyone in Moscow was on extremely short rations because they were not soldiers or necessary to the war effort. We correspondents had a special dining room where we ate and we had decent meals. We also had access to the U.S. military mission, which got supplies from Tehran, and we were able to provide the Russians who worked for us with bread and cheese and meat enough to keep them alive. Most of the other inhabitants of the hotel were Russians, so we made friends with Russian newspapermen and writers and some people in theater—all kinds of people. We didn't give a damn about politics and we hardly went to the embassy. The war was the news.

There were two briefing sessions a day in the press department of the foreign office, one at eight in the morning and the other at eleven in the evening. That was the big one, at which they gave out details of the Red Army's advances that day. There was only one problem about it for an agency man, and this was locating the points of advance on a map, because they didn't locate them for you, they just read the report off. We had practically no reference materials except for a map on the wall of the press department. You had to locate where these places were, get your dispatch written and into the censor, and then get it transmitted. So the first person to locate the day's point of advance on the map usually got the story and the headline in the *New York Times*. It was a big deal, and the competition between AP, Reuters, and UP was very keen. On several occasions there was such a struggle between correspondents to get to that map and find the location that the map would be torn down from the wall and sometimes destroyed—small riots in other words.

The censorship was very severe. We didn't complain about military censorship; it was wartime and we expected that sort of thing. But what bothered us most was the ignorance factor. The Russian censors didn't understand what we wrote and so they would cut it. This caused a lot of friction and irritation, so much so that when I left Russia, having been there about eight months, I hoped I would never have to go back there again.

I kept in touch with the news from Russia of course, working for UP in New York. I knew after Stalin's speech in early 1946 to the Supreme Soviet, and Churchill's Iron Curtain speech in Fulton, Missouri, a few weeks later, that it was going to be Cold War, and I knew that it was going to be very rough. But it didn't concern me directly because I wasn't going to be going back there.

But then, all of a sudden, out of the blue, when I went to work for the *New York Times* they said, "Russia's where we want you to go; you've got background there." Drew Middleton had been the *Times* correspondent there and when he left on vacation they wouldn't let him back in. So the *Times* hadn't had anybody there for a year and a half or something like that.

It was a totally different ballgame when I came back in '49 than it had been during the war. From the time I arrived until sometime after the death of Stalin in '53 not one person whom I had known would even say hello to me. I learned this in the very first week or so when I'd call someone up and bing, as soon as I introduced myself, they'd be right off the telephone. I'd see people I knew walking in the street and they'd look away. I quickly came to understand that if these people had any contact with me they could be just picked right up and sent off to Siberia.

The State Secrets Act was so tough that if I called the weather bureau and asked whether it was going to snow that night they couldn't tell me. The airport couldn't tell me if a plane had come in from Helsinki. Any kind of an interview from a schoolteacher to a janitor had to go through the press department and usually they just didn't set it up. There were four cities we were supposed to be able to visit but in the nearly five years I was there before Stalin's death I managed to make only two trips to Leningrad and one each to Stalingrad and Odessa. I was never given permission to go to Kiev. Once in a great great while the press department would organize a trip. When Moscow University built a new skyscraper building they took us to see it. But that was it—just the building. We were never able to get back to see any professors or students.

One thing I did immediately was to start to learn Russian. I had made no attempt during the war because initially I thought I'd be there for only a few weeks. When I went in for the *Times* I knew I was going to be there for probably three years anyway, maybe longer. I hired a series of tutors and took lessons every goddam bloody day, whacking away at the language and then studying on my own, too, directly orienting the language to learning the job, to reading the newspapers, to learning enough so I could at least conduct primitive interviews. I really had the devil on my tail. I had a translator, but I was sure, since the translators were all being arrested, that the day was going to come when I would have no translator and I'd really be on my own.

We sent our stories from the telegraph office, where there was a little cubbyhole for correspondents with some plain desks. You had to bring your own typewriter. On one side was a row of three telephone booths and at one end there was a counter with a clerk. You wrote your story in four copies, one for yourself and three for the clerk. She took those three copies back to another room where the censor was and the censor would censor the copies and then ring a buzzer or something and she'd go back and bring them out. The censor would keep one. You had one for yourself and one that you could send if it hadn't been mutilated by the censor. The clerk wouldn't do anything with your copy unless you told her to, because often when you got it back it was just in ribbons. We never even saw the censors. We could send notes to them but that was all.

So, what do you do in a situation like this? Well, you don't just sit on your tail in your office and drink, although some people did that. For one thing I subscribed to eighteen newspapers, about ten of those in Moscow and the others from the provinces. I subscribed to probably fifteen magazines, mostly literary magazines but also some technical magazines that might have science stories and things of that kind. In comparing the papers from the provinces with those in Moscow you could get a very good idea of the difference in conditions out in the country; you knew they were far behind. Whatever there was, Moscow had it. And looking at these papers you could see how little these areas had.

I also developed a series of techniques which, while not perfect, were really quite helpful in learning things that were happening in Moscow. One was to walk the streets, literally walk the streets. I had one particular walk which I took about once a week that led me through a certain number of downtown streets and past a certain number of shops and shopping areas and markets. And I followed that route religiously, going into these shops, observing how many people were in the shops, what they were buying, picking up anything I could about their clothing and general appearance. I also observed advertisements, billboards, and bulletin boards, which were sometimes just walls where people had the habit of putting up little notes—piano for sale, or bed needed, room for exchange, things like that. If there were prices mentioned I would jot them down to give me some notion of what the market might be and any changing values. I used that walk as a kind of litmus test for what might be happening—the sort of thing people would tell me if I had ordinary conversations.

And I came to know not only the shop windows but the people in the streets. And even though I wasn't consciously observing them all the time, I knew what they looked like and I knew what they should look like. It served me well. About a month after Stalin died, I was walking down Gorky Street, which is the principal street in Moscow, the Fifth Avenue if you will, and I was oppressed by a sense that there was something wrong with the street. I finally stopped at a street corner and just stood there looking at the crowd, because I had a sense it was something about the people. I couldn't get a clue until finally, just right in front of me, a man passed by and I saw on his overcoat the white threads of a military emblem which had been taken off. And I saw he didn't have his shoulder boards on. And suddenly I realized that he was wearing a uniform overcoat but the military insignia had been taken off. And I began to look then at the crowd and, lo and behold, there was hardly a uniform to be seen. And that's what I had sensed without realizing it.

Now, this may seem a trivial thing, but in the last year of Stalin's rule practically all the ministries had adopted uniforms so they could sort of blend in with the army—the coal mining ministry, the railroad administration, you name it, they all had their own uniforms. And now I suddenly realized that the uniforms had been abolished. The only people who had uniforms now were the soldiers, the real soldiers. Well, this was a fact of some significance because it reinforced what I already had suspected: the heirs of Stalin were pandering to the military and I knew just instinctively that the military didn't like other people wearing uniforms. I wrote a story about this and its political significance and most of it got through the censorship.

I would also go to the theater a great deal, even before I could understand what was going on. I used the theater as a language tool. At the start I particularly went to classic plays —Chekov, things like that— which I could read in English and then listen to in Russian. As soon as I got a little bit better I went to the contemporary plays, just to see what the propaganda lines were and to see what I could learn about everyday Russian life. Many of these plays were American spy plays. You always knew the CIA agent, with his trenchcoat and his pulled-down cap. Sometimes you'd pick up marvelous things. In one of these spy plays, one of the villains walked across the stage and everybody looked at each other because they knew he was not an American. Now, why do you supposed they knew that? His shoes squeaked. All Russian shoes squeak, so this was a giveaway, a deliberate giveaway. This was a Russian traitor!

There was really nobody in the American embassy that knew much about Russia. The embassy personnel were not permitted to go out on the streets, practically speaking, except in twos and threes because of the supposed danger of the Russians "turning" them. Everyone was suspicious of everyone else. The British and the Americans, supposedly good friends, didn't share any of their secrets, if they had any; they didn't trust one another to keep them. You have to remember that this was the worst time of the cold war and nobody wanted to show any friendship or even too much knowledge about the Russians. You played a lone hand then.

The one real exception in terms of knowing about Russia was the Israeli embassy, which was brand new at the time. It's forgotten now but the Russians were the first to recognize the new Israeli state, even ahead of the United States. The Israelis were far and away the best because every single member of the staff had been born in Russia and they all had relations there. They knew the language, they went to the synagogue, and

they knew what was happening. I couldn't quote them of course but they
became part of my background information.

So, when I put all of this together, it gave a marvelous tapestry of
what Russian life was really like, and it gave insight into what was really
happening in the country. And these were skills that served me very well.
I found when I left Moscow and began to report in this country and in
other countries that these techniques of observation and watching and
looking in ways reporters don't ordinarily do were very helpful. Even when
I was back in the United States and I went over to Brooklyn to do stories
on the street gangs there, my eye was accustomed to observing the street
and what was going on on the street and I found I could see a lot more
than some people.

It was this kind of intimate observation of the small number of facts
one had available that helped me to sense that something was happening
in the months before Stalin died. The first thing I noticed was that events
began to happen rapidly—after a long desert suddenly water was gushing
—which is to say that for two years there had been nothing but a pattern
of stated events and then suddenly toward the end of the summer of 1952
they announced the Nineteenth Party Congress. There hadn't been a party
congress since before the war, though there was supposed to be one every
three years. One of the things one learned to observe with great care was
the posting of the portraits of the leaders, because it was a stated order
that showed whether they were going up or coming down. And all of a
sudden there began to be divergences that showed clearly there was some
kind of political confusion. And then immediately after the party congress
there began to be items in the press about arrests and trials. In Georgia,
where Beria came from, all kinds of people associated with Beria were
being arrested, even though he was still in his position. And then a lot of
people in the trade networks started to be arrested down in Kiev. Since
we knew that arrests always were followed by bigger arrests, we began to
see that it might be something bigger than we had imagined.

Then, in early January, there was a little item, the most sinister item
I've ever seen in a paper anywhere. It was on the back page of *Pravda,*
announcing what came to be known as the doctors' plot. There was an
announcement of the arrest of four Jewish doctors. They were the Kremlin
doctors and they were charged with having medically mismanaged the
cases of several important generals who had died and of one or two
political people. And that was it. As soon as you saw that you knew that

something very big was happening; it was obviously the first indication of a new purge. And then bing, bing, bing, more and more of these items about arrests. By early February those few of us who were left in Moscow—two from AP, one from UP, myself and the Reuters fellow—got together to decide what we should do and whether we should get the hell out. You could just see the outline of a new purge trial which we believed had to have a foreign participant. There had to be one guy in a trenchcoat, and we figured it was going to be one of us. I decided it wasn't going to be me anyway, but that whatever happened I was going to stay there and cover the story.

When we got the news that Stalin had had a stroke it was obvious he was going to die. From then on we maintained a continuous coverage of the telegraph office and listened to the Tass broadcasts. We discovered that there was something called the Tass dictation-speed broadcast, in which news was dictated to the provincial papers by radio during the night. That broadcast was frequently where the news first appeared. So we had our chauffeurs monitoring that frequency and we took up positions inside the telegraph office. The night Stalin died we were very tense and we were all at the telegraph office. We had instructed our chauffeur—I was working with the AP men—that if he heard anything he was not to dash in— because that would give it away to the opposition—but he was just to saunter in and give us a wink and we would saunter up to the telegraph clerk and give her our dispatches.

So about 4 or 5 A.M. the chauffeur came in and as soon as we saw him we knew that that must be it. A minute later the others stormed in, making a great fuss, shouting "Need a line to London!" "Need a line to New York!" I asked for a call to Paris, which none of the agencies were using, because I had made arrangements to dictate to that office if necessary. Everybody was shouting at this poor girl to get a line up, they wanted a line, and nothing was happening. And as all this was going on I was standing watching this clerk through the little peep hole in the frosted glass and I saw a weary looking workman come along with his tools and he ripped off the back of the telephone switchboard—it was an old-fashioned plug-in switchboard—and he yanked out the main cord. I knew then there were not going to be any telephone calls out of Moscow for a good long time. What we didn't know was that the worldwide service of Tass had put the news out and everybody in the world knew about it. They just weren't letting it through from Moscow.

It's hard to say what the Russian people felt about Stalin's death. I saw plenty of old ladies crying and moaning and all that. I think they were sorry but it's also a fact that this is the traditional way they express themselves when someone dies. I know that people were stunned by this event and they couldn't really believe that Stalin could be dead. I went out in the morning to see what was happening in Red Square and I saw people standing in a big clot in the middle of the square, just kind of dazed. And they also were scared as hell of what might come after. They didn't think of themselves as having been liberated; they thought something worse would come. I think that most of them thought that Beria, the police chief, was going to take over. There were enormous lines to view Stalin's body in the so-called Hall of Columns and finally I joined one and we zig-zagged through the alleys until we got to where Stalin's body was lying in state.

Six months later or so I came back to the United States, having been told that I'd be replaced. But they didn't have a replacement ready and much against my wishes I had to agree to go back and fill in until they got somebody. It turned out to be more fun than I ever had in my whole life, really, because restrictions were all gone to the wind and I was the only person around—all the others had been pulled out—who knew what was going on. I was on page one practically every day with a marvelous story.

I traveled all over the country from one end of it to another by myself —no translator, nobody accompanying me, doing everything for myself. That really increased my fluency in the language enormously. I had to interview in Russian and all that sort of thing. I'd never taken a picture in the Soviet Union until after Stalin died—I didn't dare—but on one of my first trips I was in Samarkand in central Asia and there were just such wonderful things I couldn't resist. I walked into a shop and bought the same little camera that I carried all over. Many of the pictures I took ran with the stories I did after my return to the United States.

All of which is not to say that the heavy hand of the police wasn't still around. I got out to Siberia to the headquarters of what the KGB called their industrial division—in other words, slave labor—and they put about twenty guys on me, following me. The "taxi driver" who took me around had obviously been called into duty hastily because he had an ordinary jacket on but he still had his KGB trousers on; I recognized them by the red stripe down the side. There was barbed wire and forced labor every-where; they couldn't conceal it.

Then I got on the train to go to the Jewish autonomous region where nobody had been for twenty years and as I got on, a whole contingent of plainclothesmen got on with me. I was totally surrounded. We arrived about midnight and there were no lights on the station platform. I didn't have a clue as to where the hotel was or whether there *was* a hotel; you couldn't find out things like that. I thought, "What am I going to do?" And then I thought, "They have to go someplace; I'll follow them." They led me to the hotel, which was very primitive. Every time I went to the toilet —they had only outdoor toilets—at least two KGB people had to go along, too.

Then I discovered a very funny game. Just by chance I was coming out of the hotel with a camera around my neck and as I walked out the door I put my hand up to keep it from banging against me. Well, as I put my hand up, what had been a totally peaceful scene dissolved and five men started running in different directions to hide, thinking I was going to take their picture. I went for a walk in the park and of course they had to follow me there, too. There wasn't any place to hide except behind trees and every time I put my hand up to the camera, bing, they all fled. Finally I took a picture of one guy hiding under a bench.

It was great fun, no doubt about that.

10

JOHN D. PAULSON
Tornado!

JOHN D. PAULSON IS A SECOND-GENERATION EDITOR OF
the Fargo, N.D. *Forum*. His father moved the family to Fargo in 1916,
when Paulson was six months old, and later bought an interest in the
Forum as he rose through the editing ranks.

"Dad's philosophy was that when you've got a big story, you go after
it with everything you've got," Paulson recalls. Such homegrown wisdom
was put to the test in 1957, soon after Paulson had taken over the top job
at the paper, when a devastating tornado hit the town on an evening in
June. Fargo, then a town of 55,000 surrounded by prime ranch and farm
land in the heart of the Red River Valley, was accustomed to its share of
blizzards and other natural calamities. This tornado, however, was not only
destructive but also unusually cruel, leaving in its wake a sixty-six-block
swath of wrecked or battered buildings and 10 people dead, including six
children from a single family.

At 1:09 A.M., five hours and twenty-nine minutes after the tornado
struck, the *Forum* presses rolled, producing a paper that included two
front-page stories, a dramatic front-page photograph by staffer Cal Olson,
and more than two dozen additional stories and pictures inside the paper.
Many of the bylines, Paulson notes with satisfaction, carried the names of
photographers and others on the staff of less than forty who did not
normally serve as reporters but who jumped in to aid the team effort. For
its work, The Fargo *Forum* won a 1958 Pulitzer Prize. A portion of
Paulson's own contribution follows.

THE FARGO FORUM
June 21, 1957

FORUM EDITOR DESCRIBES RUSH TO BASEMENT AS TORNADO HITS
by
JOHN D. PAULSON

When a newspaperman is caught directly in the path of a tornado, he does just like everybody else. He gets his family into the southwest corner of the basement, stays there himself and prays that no one is hurt.

At least that's what I did. . . .

Down there in the southwest corner we just sat and waited for what was going to happen to happen. I peeked upward out of the small basement window and saw all kinds of debris sailing through the air in a northerly direction.

Then the debris began to swirl and I knew we were in the virtual center of the tornado's funnel. There were sounds of windows popping upstairs and some more solid thuds.

Then in a minute or two it was all over.

On the way upstairs for a look the first thing we saw was a back door smashed in. The kitchen was a mess, with dishes, utensils, food and broken glass scattered all around. Throughout the downstairs more windows were smashed, and rain came spitting in. A glance at the backyard showed that our two-car garage had disappeared. On the roof of the car that had been inside the garage was a two-foot square chunk of brick chimney.

There was nothing to do but get the family into the car and take them over to my parents, and report for tornado duty at The Fargo Forum.

There editors, reporters and photographers were already swinging into action, so back I went for a closer look at my own neighborhood.

11

MARY LOU WERNER FORBES
The Virginia School Integration Battle

MARY LOU WERNER STARTED AT THE WASHINGTON *EVENING Star* in 1944 as a seventeen-year-old copy girl. In 1959, she won a Pulitzer Prize for her coverage of the Virginia school crisis touched off by the state's determination to oppose school integration. "Integration anywhere means destruction everywhere," Governor J. Linsay Almond, Jr. said in January 1958 in an inaugural speech reported by Werner in the *Star*.

Working under tremendous deadline pressure, since the *Star* was an afternoon paper with five editions coming out throughout the day, Werner reported on a series of state actions and court decisions that charted the course of the ultimately unsuccessful "massive resistance" campaign. Recalling how she would be handed a court decision at ten o'clock or so in the morning and would immediately rush to a phone, she says, "Ninety percent of my stuff would be dictated, right off the top of my head. I guess there aren't many of us left who are used to doing that." Her stories show not just an ability to report accurately under deadline pressure, but also skill in explaining and interpreting events.

Thirty years later, as Mary Lou Forbes, she is now editor of the Commentary section of the *Washington Times*. A large, pleasant woman with swept back brown hair and a voice tinged with a good bit of her native Virginia, she conveys authority coupled with warmth and a sense of humor. She says she perceives her role at the *Times,* a conservative paper owned by an organization associated with the Rev. Sun Myung Moon, as providing readers with alternative perspectives to those they encounter in the more liberal *Washington Post*.

As for the name change, she says, she got married four years after winning the Pulitzer but it wasn't until the *Star* folded and she was called on to cowrite the paper's obituary that she altered her byline to Forbes. By then, she had a son old enough to take pride in his mother's work. "I thought, 'This will be something he will cherish because it's his name," she says, adding with a laugh, "and here I am now living under an assumed name."

Following is a portion of one of the stories for which Mary Lou Werner Forbes won a Pulitzer Prize.

THE EVENING STAR
January 11, 1958

ALMOND REAFFIRMS MASSIVE RESISTANCE
by
MARY LOU WERNER

RICHMOND—J. Lindsay Almond, Jr., stood by Virginia's "massive resistance" laws today as he assumed the office of Governor, and called for additional power to close any schools policed by Federal troops.

In an inaugural address bristling with States' rights oratory, the new Democratic Governor rejected any idea of "compromises," "token integration" or local control of the race question.

"To compromise means to integrate," he warned. "I find no area of compromise that might be usefully explored."

He said he could not visualize a "little integration" anyfmore than he could picture "a small avalanche or a modest holocaust."

His stand ended speculation that he might pursue a softer course than his predecessor on the school segregation issue. Some circles had interpreted his silence on certain aspects of the controversy as meaning that he might recommend some token integration as a means of warding off integration on a large scale.

As for local control, which his Republican opponents advocated in the gubernatorial campaign, Gov. Almond declared:

"I am convinced that there is not one political subdivision in Virginia where racially mixed schools can be conducted without such serious and irretrievable loss and damage to the cause of public education as to render the attempt, even on an experimental basis, all but futile."

He said he considered his election in November a clear

mandate from the voters to continue Virginia's battle against Federal encroachment, and said "to sanction any plan which would legalize the mixing of the races in our schools would violate the clear and unmistakable mandate of the people to which I earlier referred. This I cannot do."

MARY LOU WERNER FORBES:
THE STORY BEHIND THE STORY

I live in Alexandria, within a mile of where I've lived all my life. In the '30s, when I was growing up, segregation in the schools was never an issue we heard discussed among whites.

After finishing high school I began classes at the University of Maryland with the ambition of majoring in math, but my mother was a widow and we just didn't have enough money for me to continue. So I left with the intention of earning enough money to go back. I applied for a job in the accounting department of the *Evening Star*, primarily because it was at the end of the bus line that went by my home, but they laughed at the idea of a seventeen-year-old taking a job as an accountant. They said, "We do have this opportunity upstairs that you might be interested in. It's called a copy boy." That's how I got into journalism.

There were probably four or five women in the newsroom at that time, including one who covered the education beat, but no blacks. Black and white Washington were separate. Even the civic groups were separate: the whites had the Citizens Associations and the blacks had Civic Associations. The *Washington Star* each year gave a cup for outstanding civic service to the winner in each one of the two groups.

After three years, I became a reporter covering the suburbs. The paper was just beginning to cover both Virginia and Maryland in greater depth because the veterans were coming home after the war and moving out there. I remember the editor who talked to me about the reporting job said, "Well, you're not about to get married, are you?" I said, "No sir, no sir." I think maybe he scared me out of ten or fifteen years of marriage. Can you imagine being asked that today?

But you know, I always felt that it was a real challenge to disprove their notions, so I didn't resent it. I think maybe you did work harder if you were a woman, because you knew you had an image problem to overcome. Maybe some of the men resented it because they felt they had to go home to their wives and families whereas the women coming along in that era were not really expected to be married. So we had all the time in the world to give to the job.

One thing I did was to cover school board meetings. People were aware even in those days, the late '40s and early '50s, before *Brown vs. Board of Education,* that things were going to have to change. I can remember a school superintendent discussing sites for new schools and saying, "Now, don't forget, there are cases pending in the courts. We might have to make some adjustments here, we might want to think about whether this school would serve just the"—this is horrible but this is what they called them—"the darky community." So they knew. Nobody wanted to get out in front, though, which is what I believe made it inevitable that the courts did.

I was covering the Virginia General Assembly at the time the so-called massive resistance laws were passed. Right after the *Brown* decision the then governor, Tom Stanley, had very reasonable things to say, but then political considerations got involved. One of the main laws was that the minute a Negro entered a white school the school was closed. Another one was that the state would give a tuition grant to anybody who wanted to go to a private school.

Albertis Harrison, who was elected state Attorney General in 1957, and who later became governor, filed a suit as Attorney General challenging that law. The filing was accompanied by a terse announcement that the state wanted to make sure that giving state money to private individuals to go to private schools was all legally okay under the Virginia constitution. I talked to Harrison and that conversation is a good example of how you get your insights into things.

I asked Harrison, "Is this just another stalling move?" Well, he was silent for a long time. Then he said, "Don't you ever quote me on this, but let me tell you, if we've got to get rid of these laws, let me ask you something: is it better for us to get rid of them in our state court"—this case was filed in a state court and meanwhile there was a challenge of the same laws by the NAACP in the federal court—"is it better for us to get rid of them, will the people swallow it better, or do we wait for the federal court to do it?" I said, "Say no more." But that gave me the tip-off. I wrote my story to say that the State of Virginia had filed this suit and then, very quickly, I added that while some saw it as a delaying tactic, others—and

of course those "others" were no better source than Harrison—felt. . .and
then I described the issue of state versus federal action. I was the only
reporter who played it like that. The *New York Times* and the *Washington
Post* and everybody else jumped to the conventional conclusion that it was
solely a delaying tactic.

I got along with the NAACP as well as with the leadership in Virginia
and both sides talked to me to the extent they could about their court
strategies or what they believed would happen next or even beyond that.
We respected confidences in those days perhaps more than now and I
would get tips from both sides. There were some really delightful lawyers
on both sides. Spottswood Robinson was one of the NAACP attorneys, a
brilliant man, and he could really argue a case. I complimented him one
day on one of his appearances in court. One of the arguments was about
busing—whether this wouldn't lead to isolation. Robinson started talking
in court about what he called the loneliness of the Negro. "It doesn't hurt
him," he said. "He can survive it. We've survived it for years." I told him
later, "That really got me." And he said, "Oh, I use that one all the time."

Most of the stories I did on what was happening were breaking news
but I did some feature stories whenever I could. I'd go to a town, for
example, and do a piece on the mood of the town. I was also still covering
a lot of politics and I remember following around a politician one day who
was running for Congress. He was trying to deal gingerly with questions
about the school situation as he went through a very definitely lower-
income white area, I think it was actually public housing. Some young
woman, with babies squabbling around, asked him, "Well, what are you
going to do about this integration thing?" and he came up with a standard
politician's answer: "It's a real problem we've got to solve"—you know,
the whole routine—and she said, "Well, I just don't think it's right. I
could have been born"—I guess she said colored—"I could have been
born colored and I wouldn't want anybody to have laws against me." So
here was some poor lady who you'd think had nothing more on her mind
than how warm is the pablum and this is what she was saying.

No matter how hard you tried to be even-handed, it was such a
sensitive issue that people would call to complain even about how we
covered a legal decision. But we did take care to avoid inflammatory
pieces. There was a strong sense that Virginia would work its way out of
this, maybe not as fast as it should, but that if the paper did its job of
informing people they would make the right decision.

When my stories won a Pulitzer Prize it was a total surprise to me. I knew that they had been put into a lot of contests but I just hadn't paid much attention; certainly the stories were not done with any eye on a prize or anything. I'd just become assistant state editor when I won—I was in fact the first woman on the main desk—and I remember Newbold Noyes, the executive editor, said, "Boy, this makes us look stupid. Someone wins the prize and she's an editor."

I continued to be an editor at the *Star* until it closed, and I watched what happened with integration over the years. Of course there were a lot of private schools started by white parents that continue to this day. But on the whole I feel things came out fairly well. My son Jimmy went to public schools in Virginia in the lower grades and he moved very easily with kids of all races. I remember at one point he was the only white kid on a basketball team.

On the thirtieth anniversary of *Brown vs. Board of Education* it was suggested that I go back down to Prince Edward County to do a story for the paper. I was tremendously impressed by both the white and black educators there and the local people. This didn't mean that somebody had waved a wand, but there were people within Virginia who were committed to making integration work. Carl Rowan, the columnist, also went down there quite independently of me and it turned out that we both sort of came to the same conclusion: at least they've made a beginning.

PART
IV

THE SIXTIES

□

12

DAVID HALBERSTAM
Vietnam—Sliding Toward Disaster

WHEN DAVID HALBERSTAM WENT TO VIETNAM AS A *NEW York Times* correspondent in 1962, the United States had thousands of advisers in that country but had not yet committed ground troops. What Halberstam did, along with a handful of other American journalists, was to document the failure of a military and political strategy that would lead in the end to the loss of 57,000 American lives, one million Vietnamese lives, and the tearing apart of both U.S. and Vietnamese societies.

During the fifteen months he spent in Vietnam, Halberstam, who was born in 1934, lived through a period of growing turmoil that culminated in the overthrow of Vietnamese President Ngo Dinh Diem. Because his reports were so at odds not just with what the administration was saying, but also with what many other journalists were saying, Halberstam and the *Times* came in for frequent criticism. For his work, Halberstam was awarded a Pulitzer Prize in international reporting in 1964. AP Vietnam correspondent Malcolm Browne was also awarded a Pulitzer Prize for international reporting in that year.

To be sure, the meaning of U.S. involvement in Vietnam was not quite as clear then as it is now. In a book called *The Making of a Quagmire,* which he wrote upon his return from Vietnam, Halberstam argued that Vietnam was "perhaps one of only five or six nations in the world that is truly vital to U.S. interests," and that withdrawal would mean that "throughout the world the enemies of the West will be encouraged to try insurgencies like the one in Vietnam."

Halberstam says now of his views at that time, "We were all in transition. I thought we probably owed the Vietnamese a chance, particularly because they'd had such an incompetent government for so long. But I was just so dubious, and growing more dubious all the time." He adds, referring to his work and that of his colleagues in Vietnam, "We were the point men at an almost historical watershed in the history of America, a time when America's power carried it too far, from a legitimate kind of anti-communism based upon lessons of pre-World War II, and lessons of dealing with the Soviet Union at a time of containment, to a situation in an underdeveloped world where nationalism, not communism, was the most important thing."

In the years since Vietnam, Halberstam has written a number of books including *The Best and the Brightest,* a portrait of the men behind America's Vietnam policy.

Following is an excerpt from one of a range of dispatches for which Halberstam was awarded a Pulitzer Prize.

THE NEW YORK TIMES
November 24, 1963

VIETNAM'S LEADERS FACE A TOUGH CHALLENGE
by
DAVID HALBERSTAM

SAIGON, Nov. 23--The Mekong Delta stretches out green and lush at this time of year, inviting in both its richness and simplicity. It is, says one friend, "Like nothing you have ever seen: the farmer, his wife, the rice, the coconuts, pineapples, oranges, ducks, chickens, dogs and pigs, the children fishing in canals and riding the water buffaloes"—he paused and added: "Just like a page out of the Bible."

But there is trouble in paradise and once an American flying over it in a helicopter pointed out the window and said, "Just as far as the eye can see: miles and miles of discontent."

Today in this discontented paradise the most vicious war in today's world shuttles back and forth in front of peasant huts, troops moving along tree lines are wary both of the enemy and of aroused water buffaloes, and often, as they approach, peasants file from the villages wearing their Sunday best to distinguish them from the guerrillas.

The stakes are high in this rich and fertile land. Where the Communists had been making frighteningly successful inroads, the new Government has answered with a major challenge and the lines are drawn. The stakes could hardly be higher, for what happens here may decide not only what happens eventually in this country but perhaps what happens in much of Southeast Asia as well.

There is nothing simple or easy about this region nor, having joined this challenge, is there any inexpensive way out for either side. The price this year is likely to be steep in blood. For this war is not as former rulers of Vietnam said, in its final quarter-hour. Rather, in the delta, it has barely begun.

Or worse. For it appears unmistakably that there has been a slow and subtle erosion of the Government position and initiative: that the Vietcong have similarly become better armed, more aggressive and have slowly undermined the Government's position with the population.

For it is one of the bitter realities of the past year that it is the Government's side which has repeated its mistakes, inevitably to the benefit of the guerrillas, while the guerrillas rarely made the same mistake twice; it is the Government side which created an attitude of almost willful self-delusion on developments here, and, what is particularly bitter to Westerners, it is the Communist side which reacted more flexibly to changing developments and which has so far shown the most motivation and discipline. . . .

Some people—neutralists, French, Communists—feel that this is a war forced on the Vietnamese by the Americans and that there is a subsurface desire on the part of the Vietnamese to make a deal with Hanoi at almost any price.

Yet others, Vietnamese and Americans, believe that this is not true, that there is still a capacity on the part of the Vietnamese to fight well if they are well-led and if they have something to fight for. What will be proved in the delta will be how well they are led and whether they have something worth fighting for.

Portrait of Joseph Pulitzer by John Singer Sargent.

A meeting of the Pulitzer Board, c. late 1930s. From the left: Ralph Pulitzer (son of
Joseph Pulitzer), *The New York World;* Frank R. Kent, *The Baltimore Sun;* an un-

(BELOW) Pulitzer Prize Board members, 1988. Seated from left: Frederick T.C. Yu,
acting dean of the Graduate School of Journalism (ex-officio); Michael I. Sovern, president, Columbia University; Roger W. Wilkins, Pulitzer Prize Board chairman, senior
fellow, Institute for Policy Studies; David A. Laventhol, president, Times Mirror
Company; Robert C. Christopher, Pulitzer Prize Board secretary. Standing, from the
left: Eugene L. Roberts Jr., executive editor, *The Philadelphia Inquirer;* Burl Os-
borne, president and editor, *The Dallas Morning News;* Howard Simons, curator, Nie-

identified aide; Nicholas Murray Butler, president, Columbia University; Arthur M. Howe, *Brooklyn Daily Eagle.*

man Foundation, Harvard University; Claude Sitton, editorial director and vice president, *The News & Observer/The Raleigh Times;* Peter R. Kann, associate publisher, *The Wall Street Journal;* Michael Gartner, editor, *The Daily Tribune,* (Ames, Iowa) and General News Executive, Gannett Co.; Russell Baker, columnist, *The New York Times;* Charlotte Saikowski, chief of Washington bureau, *The Christian Science Monitor;* C.K. McClatchy, editor and chairman of the board, McClatchy Newspapers; Meg Greenfield, editorial page editor, *The Washington Post;* James F. Hoge, Jr., publisher, *The New York Daily News.*

Joe Pineiro/Columbia University

Members of a Pulitzer screening jury at work, c. 1950.

Herbert Bayard Swope, left, standing with Alfred Gwynne Vanderbilt
at Belmont Park in 1941, years after he won his Pulitzer Prize. Swope was chairman
of the New York State Racing Commission at the time.

Walter Duranty, center, talks with Kenneth Durant, Tass representative, on the left, and A. Bernard Moloney, of Reuters, on the right, at a 1936 lunch.

Homer Bigart

Hanson Baldwin

World War II Associated Press
correspondent Daniel De Luce
celebrates on Anzio beachhead
after receiving word that
he had won a Pulitzer Prize.

Edwin Guthman, flanked by his wife and his mother.

John D. Paulson

Harrison Salisbury

Mary Lou Werner Forbes

UPI/Bettmann Newsph

David Halberstam

Paul Conrad

Ed Maker/The Denver Post

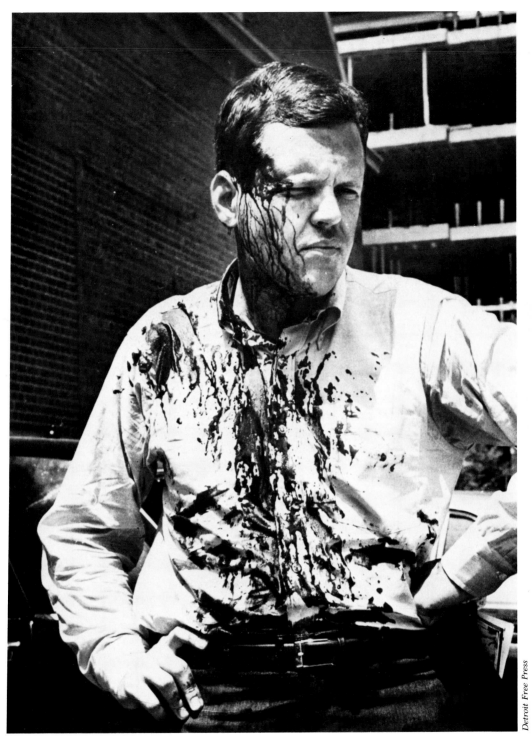

William Serrin, moments after he was injured during the 1967 Detroit riot.

Detroit Free Press

Gene Miller, left, shares a moment of delight at the news of his 1976 Pulitzer Prize with *Miami Herald* executive editor Larry Jinks.

(RIGHT TOP) Stanley Forman, left, celebrates winning his 1976 Pulitzer Prize with *Boston Herald American* publisher Robert C. Bergenheim.

(RIGHT BOTTOM) Joe Hughes greets San Diego residents from atop a *Tribune* billboard.

Boston Herald American

Albert Scardino, left, and his wife, Marjorie, peruse a copy of *The Georgia Gazette* while A. Preston Russell, a Savannah physician who is a fixture at historic galas, looks on.

(AT RIGHT) Edna Buchanan in the *Miami Herald* newsroom minutes after hearing that she won a 1966 Pulitzer Prize.

value to us because he went on every major operation. He would take us whenever we wanted to go and even if we couldn't go on an operation we could go out to his company later and get a briefing. One time we were out at his company headquarters when some military investigators came and he hid us in his tent. Finally an Army officer came out and told him to stop taking us and he told them, "Get the fuck out of my company. They're my helicopters and they're my friends. They can go anytime they want."

I think I toted up something like fifty-six combat missions that I'd gone on. I remember what it was like: getting up at 4 A.M. and drinking that awful army coffee and trying to eat breakfast. You knew you had to eat breakfast but it was too early and you were about to go into battle so you were nervous and tense. And then the thrill when we took off, going up above the Mekong delta and the beauty of dawn rising on the delta— the utter glory, the biblical sense of it. And then you'd get out and your mouth was so dry and you were in water up to your waist. It was terrifying. I felt very large and very vulnerable. You weren't sitting on the sidelines; you were risking your life. But you'd never felt so alive.

As time went on, more and more people sought us out, told us things. In the spring of 1963 Horst Faas, the brilliant AP photographer, and I rented a house together, a large villa belonging to a German foreign service officer, and people used to come there all the time. They were mostly Army officers whom we had met earlier in the field, and now when they came to Saigon for a couple of days, they looked us up. And they were very straight with us. We pretty much worked out of the UPI office in downtown Saigon and anybody who came by there, we'd invite them out there for dinner and every night there would be six or eight people and we would just find out everything that was going on all over the country.

One of the problems in Vietnam was that a lot of the struggle was really generational. Our own editors were produced by World War II. They were used to generals telling the truth and the United States being on the good side: our soldiers handed out chewing gum and the other guys did massacres. A lot of our older journalistic colleagues, too, were unwilling to see that this was a different kind of war, that battlefield valor was not enough—that you could win a given set-piece battle and still lose the war.

There was also the Washington factor. You have to understand that most of our colleagues in Washington were still playing the Kennedy game and not wanting to put distance between themselves and this glistening Kennedy world, and they did not want to lose invitations to dinner. I remember coming back in '64 and one rather senior correspondent turned to me and he said, "I'd like you to know that I defended you at a dinner party last night." I thought, "Fuck you, I don't need you to defend me." He said it in such a pompous way—the insider.

There was also another thing operating: some journalists were very profoundly affected by the McCarthy period and were unwilling to admit it, but they were never again going to get near a situation where they might be accused of being soft on communism. I graduated from Harvard the year after McCarthy was censured so the burden of that did not weigh very heavily on me or reporters of my generation. But we all were affected in various ways. Our military reporting was very good—almost perfect in fact. But our political reporting wasn't as good as it should have been in an historic sense, that is, in connecting what was going on with the French Indochina war and to the comparable rot and collapse of a feudal society in China, and the reason was that the kind of people who would have been our best sources had been devastated by the McCarthy era. You just didn't have anybody in the entire State Department who was on location who had any background in Asia; they had been wiped out. A reporter is only as good as his sources and our military sources were much better than our political ones.

My editors at the *Times* were very nervous on the issue of anti-communism. Here once again was a *New York Times* reporter saying that the anti-communism struggle was not going well and that the plucky little anti-communist dictator was not winning the war. They were also uneasy about what was a clear decision on my part to go to sources who did not have titles and whose names could not be used. I kept saying, "If I give you the name of that colonel in my story he won't be a colonel anymore." They wanted stories in which I was pessimistic to have quotes from some high official in Saigon. But it was the *Catch-22* of Vietnam—the only people who would be quoted by name in dispatches were the ones who said we were winning the war. I suppose it would have been like Ben Bradlee, the editor of the *Washington Post,* asking Bob Woodward and Carl Bernstein to name Deep Throat in one of their early Watergate stories.

But on the whole the editors were very good. They took an enormous amount of abuse from the Kennedy people and from the Defense Department. Punch Sulzberger had his first meeting with Kennedy in 1961 shortly after he had taken over as publisher of the paper. He went over to the White House very nervous, accompanied by Scotty Reston. He said to Reston, "What do I say?" and Reston told him, "Don't worry Punch, he's going to ask you about your kids and then you ask him about his kids."

So they walked in and the first thing Kennedy said was, "What do you think of your young man in Saigon?" "I like him very much." "You don't think that he's a little too close to the story, do you?" "Oh no, no." "And you weren't thinking of transferring him to Paris or Rome?" "No." Right at that time I was supposed to go on some vacation to Hong Kong and the *Times* told me "Do not go," because they didn't want Kennedy to think that they had responded to the pressure. When I came back to the United States I asked Punch about the incident and he confirmed what had happened.

I think one of the most interesting things about Vietnam was the change in men like Ben Bradlee. I think Ben is the best and most important editor of his generation. And I could tell the first time or two that I met Ben, in 1965 and 1966, that he was very uneasy with me, wary of what I had done in Vietnam. His own values were set in World War II, and he was probably closer to Jack Kennedy in those days than he was to working reporters. I think that whole period was jarring enough to him that he was really very good when Carl Bernstein and Bob Woodward came along with Watergate. We were the tripwire for Watergate—for the realization that it's not just mayors in small towns in Mississippi who will lie, but generals, presidents, secretaries of state and secretaries of defense. We knew even then we were onto something important but we were still learning ourselves at the very moment we were doing it. We were in this brand new territory where there were no road maps.

In the end, what I learned was to trust my instincts. You get out there and you're covering a very, very big story and everybody in the world says, "We're winning the war," but you and a handful of friends and your sources believe you're losing it. And you work very hard and it's all you think about day and night and eventually you forget what famous people or people more senior than you say and you trust yourself.

When Mal Browne and I won the Pulitzer Prize it was as if the Supreme Court of our own profession had ruled in our favor. There was a special pleasure to winning that year, I think, though I still think Neil Sheehan should have shared it, too. In those days the board was very traditional so it was an unusual prize to win for reporting that was unusually iconoclastic. It legitimized what we had done. But we didn't really need the prize to know that what we had done was important. I think we all knew in Vietnam that we were at an historic place at an historic time, and that journalism mattered there: that it was a place where you made journalistic judgments and that you yourself were going to be judged.

13

PAUL CONRAD
A Cartoonist's View of the Kennedy Years and Beyond

HE'S A TALL MAN, STRONGLY BUILT, WITH A LONG FACE AND a jutting chin. His reputation is that of a dragon slayer in cartoonist's clothing, a man who can make the high and mighty turn pale—or more likely apoplectic—over breakfast. But in person, Paul Conrad seems, well, amiable. Stretching down to pat the family cat, who is snoozing at his feet in the warm California sunshine, Conrad makes it clear that anger toward wrongdoing and injustice is not something that colors his whole existence; rather it is the spirit that propels his work.

"If you were to stay angry all the time, you couldn't live your life," he says. But in order to do what he does, Conrad says, "you have to care, you have to have a gut reaction to what you read, what happens around you."

The results of such "gut reactions" have been delighting and infuriating readers for forty years, ever since Conrad, who was born in 1924, finally abandoned thoughts of a career as a bass player in a dance band and went to work for the *Denver Post*. There, he picked up his first Pulitzer Prize in 1964 before moving to the *Los Angeles Times*, where he collected two more, in 1971 and 1984.

Conrad's nationally syndicated cartoons display a combination of wit, strong opinion, and skillful drawing, as exemplified in a drawing done during the Vietnam conflict. It shows a father in a hard-hat nonplussed by his discovery that the peacenik hippie he is about to clobber with a bat is none other than his own son. The same mix of artistic and political sensibilities is evident in a series of sculptures done by Conrad over the past ten years. These sculptures, primarily political figures, but also including a crucifixion and a nuclear explosion, share space with paintings and photographs in the Conrads' home outside Los Angeles.

In addition to his Pulitzers, Conrad acquired what he considers another designation of note when he was named to President Richard Nixon's White House "enemies list." Later, he got his own back when he was appointed to the Richard M. Nixon chair at Whittier College, an honor that involved his giving a series of lectures on political cartooning at the former president's alma mater.

The passing of years hasn't smoothed the sharp edges of the Conrad sense of humor. In 1989, he was invited, along with several other cartoonists, to have lunch with President George Bush at the White House.

PROFILE IN COURAGE

Paul Conrad/The Denver Post

A quiet meditation on the life and death of John Kennedy
helped Conrad win a 1964 Pulitzer Prize.

"Nobody was asking any serious questions and I sort of tuned out and then I heard someone say to the President something about, 'Now you serve us hardballs, softballs, and beachballs,'" Conrad recalls. "I didn't even know what he was talking about. So I said, 'Mr. President, speaking of beachballs, how's the vice-president doing?'" Retelling the anecdote with obvious relish, Conrad adds, "I'll never be invited back."

Below are two of Conrad's prizewinning cartoons, one from his first Pulitzer entry and one from his third.

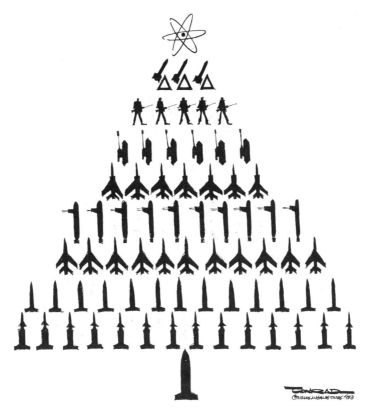

Conrad won a third Pulitzer in 1984 for a series of cartoons
that included one on the theme of weapons proliferation.

PAUL CONRAD:
THE STORY BEHIND THE STORY

My father was a railroad man. While we were growing up he was a city freight agent in Des Moines, Iowa. He had a great sense of humor about everything but religion and he could have been a very good painter, but my mother didn't think being an artist was any way to try to support a family.

I was brought up Catholic, and while it probably has had an effect on the way I view the world, the most important thing I got out of it was a sense of discipline, of how to proceed with things, of how one act is related to another. I loved Latin; it's that sense of order again. In high school I translated the Aeneid and Homer and Ovid, which for a high school kid was pretty remarkable.

I went in the army in 1942 and when I came back four years later I went to college and majored in art. I didn't have any thoughts about cartooning—I knew already that I was not a fine artist but I didn't know what else to do—until one day I was talking to Charlie Carroll, the editor of the Iowa University college paper. He complained that the paper wasn't getting any good political cartoons from the news syndicates and he said, "Con, why don't you think about cartoons?" I figured, "Why not? So Charlie and I did a little research and we decided what subjects to do and pretty soon I was appearing every day.

By the time I graduated I had a thick portfolio that I sent out to Palmer Hoyt at the *Denver Post*. He said, "Come on out when you graduate," so I did, and after about three months of retouching photos I started drawing cartoons. Then in 1964 I came out here to the *Los Angeles Times*. I've been lucky; everything has always just kind of fallen into place like that.

There's no one way that I get my ideas. Some ideas just fall into your lap; the minute you read two paragraphs of a news story you know exactly where you're going. But sometimes, especially in the dog days of August and September, it can be pretty hard coming up with fresh ideas. I do six cartoons a week which is probably one or two too many. I'd cut back but I don't know what day I'd drop. I never have anything in reserve because if a cartoon was good enough to hold onto, I'd run it. I just work better under deadline. On vacation I don't have an idea to my name.

I would work at home if I could and fax my cartoons in and save myself the agony of those commutes. But I've found through the years that I'm a people person. I go in to the paper and I do a rough sketch and take it around to all the people that are working and I shove it in front of their faces and see their reaction. If they like it, fine. If there's an objection, I ask why. One thing I try hard to do is to cut out as much verbiage as possible because as far as I'm concerned the best cartoon is one that has no words at all. Sometimes it takes me all day to do a cartoon, one rough after another, after another, after another. If it doesn't work with the people at the *Times* then there's usually no sense in doing it in the paper because a whole lot of other people won't have any idea what it's about either.

After I've got the idea, the rest is just technique. One thing that's really helped in that regard is sculpture, which I started doing about ten years ago. When you've been drawing in black and white, pretty soon the lines get stale. So I do these sculptures and all of a sudden I know what the roundness of a thing is, what the holistic measure of it is. And so the line gets better. I'd be the last to say what I do is fine art; for me the art is absolutely secondary to what you have to say.

When notables die, people like Horowitz, Jean-Paul Sartre, Helen Keller, even people such as Bing Crosby and Lucille Ball, I try very hard to do something that really captures them because those people meant a lot to an awful lot of people. When John Kennedy died, I was absolutely stricken, as everyone was. He was such a marvelous man. He could speak —God, he could speak. The Berlin Wall, Robert Frost at the inauguration, all so beautiful, and great talents going into the White House—it was just class. And then to have it absolutely wiped out. I didn't know which way to go on a cartoon, just how to handle it. I found it very difficult at that point to put anything together. It seemed to me that his writing of the book "Profiles in Courage" was one of the nicest, most courageous things that he had done. So that's where I got the idea for the cartoon that I drew.

When Helen Keller died, I did her touching God's face, like Michelangelo, touching his cheek. I loved that one. I sweated a long time on it because when you're fooling around with Michelangelo, then the execution becomes really important. For I.F. Stone I did him and Socrates toasting each other—to truth! For Vladimir Horowitz I turned his head into a grand piano.

The Horowitz cartoon is an example of how whatever I do seems to offend some group. I got a letter after I did that one signed by around twenty Jewish people saying, "Conrad is making fun of the Jewish nose." I get an average of twenty or so letters a day, usually opposed to something I've done. I read most of them because you've got to find out what the public thinks, and I answer all the ones that need it. I've also gotten a few death threats, I can't even remember now about what. And I've been sued from time to time. The *Times* has been marvelous about that. They've absolutely stood behind me.

When Reagan was governor of California, I developed this character called Reagan Hood, which Reagan really detested, so he'd call Otis Chandler, the publisher, and complain. After awhile Otis told people to say he wasn't there. So then Nancy started calling. Finally, Otis told me, he wouldn't take calls from either of them. At one point the paper did run a disclaimer, about five lines of very small type, explaining that the editorial opinions of the *Times* were represented in the editorials and not in a cartoon, the letters, or anything else. The paper also got a lot of complaints about my work during Watergate. Some of my cartoons were rather harsh. I still feel that pressure of one sort or another had something to do with the decision to move me from the editorial page to the op-ed page, though Otis Chandler told me that was absolutely not the case.

Lately, the biggest group to complain is the Jewish Defense League, because of what I've been saying about Israel and the Palestinians. As far as I'm concerned, what the Israeli army is doing is wrong. The JDL has picketed in front of our house four or five times and they've presented me with two pigs, one at home and one at the *Times*. They got together a demonstration of about three or four hundred people and they marched around the *Times* all day saying, "Conrad is another Hitler."

I'm also getting a lot of static on abortion, especially because the anti-abortion people remember when I took a different position and they can't understand why I've changed. I was with the anti-abortion people for a long, long time but finally, about three years ago, I heard Justice Brennan of the Supreme Court explaining his position and that got me to thinking. I got out all the clips and everything on *Roe vs. Wade* and finally I realized that, given the choice of the state or the individual, there's no choice, you have to choose the individual, because the individual will live with the decision and the state doesn't live with anything. So I had to change my position and I just did it, period.

My best critic is my wife, Kay. We generally agree on things—if you think I'm a radical you should see her—but she never hesitates to tell me when she doesn't like something. I remember one time when our four kids were quite small and I was describing a cartoon I'd done that she thought was a little unfair. She turned to me and said, "You bastard." The kids looked at me bug-eyed.

Social conscience was an evolving thing for me. I don't think I had much of a political conscience during the Second World War. I was on Okinawa when they dropped the bomb and if there was anyone who raised an objection I didn't hear it. We'd been over there for about a year and a half and we didn't want any more of that; the bomb made perfect sense to me. Isn't that terrible? But I was a kid then. I did begin to realize during the war that there were a great many injustices but I wasn't sure what you do to try to rectify them. And then suddenly Charlie Carroll came along with his idea about editorial cartoons.

I call myself a liberal. It's not a dirty word. Some people might think that I'm a limousine liberal, living in a nice house and all that, but I don't think it's necessary to live with the homeless to sympathize with them. Maybe that's a rationalization, probably it is. I should probably sell this house and live in a garage. But I'm not ready for that yet.

When the Vietnam War started, my opposition at first was based on my thinking that it wasn't going to work; that the war was strategically dumb. But later on it became a personal thing and a moral thing. When my kid Jamie was sixteen I said, "We've got to work fast on this and get it over with because I can't see Jamie going into this war." And then, pretty soon, all you had was Spanish Americans and blacks doing the fighting and that was just absolutely morally wrong. I think my concern about civil rights carried on more or less from what was going on in Vietnam. I couldn't tell you which one—opposition to the war or the civil rights movement—came first for me.

Over time I found out that it is possible to make a difference on social issues. Winning the Pulitzers gave me a justification to keep doing what I've been doing but to work my damnedest to do it even better. I'll keep at it as long as I have something to say.

14

WILLIAM SERRIN
The Detroit Riot

BILL SERRIN WAS TWENTY-EIGHT YEARS OLD WHEN HE COV-
ered the July 1967 Detroit riots for the *Detroit Free Press*. One of the first
newspaper reporters on the scene, he was also one of the first casualties,
his head cut open by a flying bottle. Even now, recalling the incident, he
gingerly touches his hair at the spot where the scar remains. "Scared?"
Serrin responds when questioned about how he felt during those wild few
days. "Yeah, I suppose, but when you're young, and honestly, when you're
having a great deal of fun as a journalist, you're not scared."

Serrin was also one of three reporters who spent a month after the
riot was over researching the deaths of the forty-three people who had
been killed. The team concluded that most of the victims need not have
died, and that many had done so as a result of improper or indiscriminate
use of weapons by national guardsmen and local police.

For its work, the *Free Press* was awarded a 1968 Pulitzer Prize. In its
citation, the *Free Press* was cited for both the "brilliance of its detailed
spot news staff work and its swift and accurate investigation into the
underlying causes of the tragedy."

For Serrin, the riot was a watershed experience, leading him to
develop a profound distrust of authorities and to question his own goals in
life. In this regard, Serrin stands with many people of his own generation,
black and white, who were permanently changed by the experiences they
underwent in the civil rights struggle and later, the antiwar movement.
Cracking jokes and spinning stories by the hour, Serrin is nonetheless an
intensely serious man who keeps trying to understand more fully the
events that he, and the country, have lived through.

In the years since Detroit, Serrin has worked as a free-lancer, as the
labor reporter for the *New York Times,* and as an author. "In all that I've
done since Detroit, I've really tried to do people," Serrin says. "One of the

big things that's wrong with American journalism is that we're covering the wrong stuff. We shouldn't just cover institutions; we should cover stuff from the bottom up."

Following is a portion of one of William Serrin's articles that formed part of the coverage for which the *Detroit Free Press* was awarded a Pulitzer Prize.

DETROIT FREE PRESS
July 30, 1967

COULD QUICKER ACTION, OR STRONGER ACTION, HAVE PREVENTED IT?

by
WILLIAM SERRIN

At 9 o'clock last Sunday morning, anarchy reigned on Twelfth St.

Police raced madly around in squad cars, trying to keep looters from stores, mobs from forming, young thugs from throwing rocks, always unsuccessful. Other police stayed at the intersections, openly angry because they were being stoned and were the targets of the most vile obscenities. Because of lack of numbers and orders, they could not enter combat. . . .

That was how it was before the riot spread, a time when the riot might have been prevented. That was how it was before it became the most costly Negro disturbance in American history—more costly than Watts, Hough, Harlem, Tampa, Newark—before it ended four days later, leaving at least 39 dead, 5,000 homeless, and at least $200 million in property damage.

Postmortems are easy, of course, conducted at a distance from snipers, fires and rock throwers in the air-conditioned newspaper offices, television studios, and committee rooms in Washington, Lansing and City-County Building. It is easy to criticize police Commissioner Ray Girardin, Mayor Cavanagh, the National Guard.

But one nagging thought refuses to go away: Perhaps the riot could have been prevented. . . .

Of Negro leadership, it is fair to say there was none.

The Negroes who enjoy the term leader—and thus gain access to such powers as Mayor Cavanagh, Girardin, the Common

Council, newspapers, the broadcast media, the annual Negro ban-quets—were useless in this crisis.

Many on-the-scene observers believe that no more than 100 (or perhaps 50) Negroes—teachers, local ministers, foremen in factories, mothers, storeowners, athletes—could have quelled the riot in its early stages by moving through the crowds, talking to residents, saying they were foolish, asking them to go home.

It does not seem demanding to suggest such a task force should have been organized months ago, ready for mobilization at a moment's notice. . . .

"This thing was mishandled by police and Cavanagh," says one white merchant. "When the police were told not to do any-thing out of the ordinary, the people saw that, and they went wild."

Another says:

"It didn't just start because they raided a drinking place. It started because the police just stood there when the looting started."

Girardin and Cavanagh feared shooting looters would pro-voke other Negroes at the scene. . . .

No one can be sure, of course, what actions might have prevented the outbreaks.

It is true, however, that prudent steps might have been taken before the riot began sweeping across Detroit.

Of such omissions, a riot was made.

WILLIAM SERRIN:
THE STORY BEHIND THE STORY

I grew up in Saginaw, which is a working class town. My dad was a baker. In the 1880s Saginaw was the lumber capital of the world, but you wouldn't know it now, because if you drive there from Detroit you won't see any trees; they cut them all down. After the lumber era they started making GM steering gears there.

The Saginaw River divides the town into two parts: east side and west side. Blacks live on the east side—Stevie Wonder's from Saginaw— and whites on the west side. Blacks never came on our side of town. I went to Arthur Hill High School; the blacks went to Saginaw High. So Arthur Hill's arch rival was Saginaw High, white versus black essentially. During the war my mother got a job testing machine guns so we had a black maid and that was my only association with black people other than sports.

I went to Central Michigan University. I didn't really want to go there, I wanted to go to the University of Michigan, but Michigan was regarded as an upper-class school and my father, being a working class guy, didn't think that you could send your kids there. I was in ROTC and I came out a lieutenant and was in the infantry in Korea in the early 1960s.

Korea really changed me a lot. I had wanted to go to law school but after Korea I was sort of infused with the idea of changing things and I didn't think I could do that in law very effectively. So when I got out of the army in 1964 I cast around and I decided that the only way I could see to write and to make some money was in journalism. I got into a trainee program of the Booth newspaper chain, and after a year of that I was hired by the *Saginaw News*. Anything you did there that could be perceived as remotely liberal could get you in trouble. I got to be friends with some liberal ministers and priests at the time when civil rights actions were just beginning and I remember writing something that I guess could have been regarded as positive about this one minister, an activist kid of guy, and after that I was sort of suspect by certain editors there.

What I really wanted to do was to go to the *Detroit Free Press*. This one time I was out covering some people picketing the Saginaw Board of Realtors, saying that they were not giving houses to black people, and suddenly this old car, maybe it was a Ford Falcon, pulls up. And out of it comes this guy who looks like a big bear, with big moustaches, and he takes his reporter's notebook out of his pocket and I think, "Hey, Big Time." It was Van Sauter, who was then a reporter for the *Free Press*. Later he became president of CBS News. And I thought, "I've got to get to the *Free Press* and hang out with these guys. These guys are *good*."

I finally got a job on the *Free Press* in March of 1966. The *Free Press* was a great place to work. It was the flagship paper of the Knight newspapers, or at least we always thought of it as the flagship. The editors liked good writing and Derick Daniels, who was then the assistant executive editor, had a good eye for talent. There was Van Sauter, who had his desk in the corner with a lamp and a rug, and Ellen Goodman, who became a syndicated columnist, and Kurt Luedtke, who is off doing movies now, and George Walker, who later wrote a novel, and a lot of others. There was great competition: Ellen Goodman would knock off some piece, or Van Sauter would, or another fine writer, Barbara Stanton, and you would have to do something to beat them. And we also had a great sense of competition with the *Detroit News*. The deadline was six o'clock and about 6:30 we'd all step over to the Detroit Press Club and have a couple beers before going home and the guys from the *News* would come in and you'd tell them, "I'm going to kick your ass tomorrow."

There were a couple black people on the paper but it was essentially a white paper and not tuned into the Detroit black community at all. We weren't afraid to go into the community—we would all go to the clubs to hear jazz and we felt quite safe—but we weren't really involved with what was going on there. And certainly the establishment of Detroit was worse: Detroit's leadership, including most of the newspaper executives, lived outside of town so their view of Detroit was from the freeway coming in and going out. When things blew up the *Free Press* was caught as short as any other institution in town. I've just finished reading a book about Dr. King and I keep thinking "How could I have been so dumb?" It was a blind period in America—although I suspect we're just as blind now.

At the time of the riot I was living in Pontiac with my in-laws. My wife had died and I had a little daughter. I was working that Sunday when it started. All reporters should try to work on Sundays because a lot of people don't want to work then and you get great stories. I was driving the twenty-five miles from Pontiac and I remember hearing on the radio that there was a racial disturbance on 12th Street. Twelfth Street was a semi-legendary Detroit street, a black street, lots of clubs and stuff. So I raced down to the office and the Sunday editor said, "Get down to 12th Street."

So I got there about ten o'clock in the morning and I was the first reporter there—there must have been some radio types and stuff but I was the first real reporter there—and there were cops all over the joint. So it was great. Honestly. Let's be honest, as a journalist, it was great. Cop-lines up and down the street, the cops all back there, the black guys down over here. So I figured, "Hey, I'm not going to stay here behind the lines," and I started to walk toward the black guys. I remember the cops said, "Don't go down there," but I wasn't afraid.

So I went down and I was talking to black people, where the story was, and getting some quotes like you're supposed to. There had been a lot of stuff between the cops and the black community before this and the cops had hit this blind pig—an illegal club—during the middle of the night and it was regarded in the black community as "Enough's enough." It was very hot, too, and this thing just exploded. By late morning, I think a lot of people thought the damn thing was under control. But then it just kept going. Once it got to be two or three o'clock and people started torching stuff and throwing firebombs it just took off. I remember John Conyers, the congressman, came and got up on a car with a bullhorn and he was on that car about thirty seconds and people were just yelling "Get him out of there." And Charlie Diggs, he was the other congressman, they didn't even let him get up. They thought better of Conyers; at least they let him get up on the car.

People were being nice to me and some were telling me I should get out of there but I wasn't really worried. I went into a store and called some stuff into the desk and told them, "This is a full-scale riot, you'd better get some people out here; it is starting to go." When I came out these guys from across the street just let loose with this barrage of stuff: bricks and bottles and potatoes, and I got cut in the head. I don't know whether it was because it was me, a white guy, or not. I had this very snappy blue blazer on, looking very good, but they creamed me. So I ran up about two blocks to the police lines and got back behind the lines and our photographer took me to the hospital. I got sewn up in the hospital and I was out of action for awhile. There's still a scar where I got some stitches. Then I went back to the newsroom.

By now it was about five o'clock and the town was being torched. The editors told me to go home but I wouldn't do it. I wasn't going to let them take my story away from me. This was *my* goddam story. So I went back out and I was lucky again. We knew the national guard was coming but we didn't know where they were going to go, so I sort of wandered into this high school and pretty soon I saw the guard coming in, tanks and jeeps and weapons. So I got that and called that in. I interviewed the national guard general, this big fat general, and I threw a little military jargon at him because I was trying to cozy up to him and he kind of thought I was one of them.

I remember him saying to me, "Serrin, how do you handle niggers?" I'm going, "Well, I don't know sir, how do you handle them?" And he says, "Goddam machine guns, Serrin, we're going to get tough. These niggers, they've had it now." He was going on and on like this. I wrote all of this down and I thought, "Jesus, this is incendiary," so when I called it in I changed it and I said the general said they're going to use maximum force, words like that. My future wife, Judy, was an intern then and they had put her to work doing rewrite. That was the first time I ever talked to her. I remember she laughed at me because she knew I was giving her garbage. Would I do it again? Probably not. If some general is so stupid he wants to say that, then put it in the paper.

The riot was racial, no question about it. White cops killing black people, that was racial. And on the other side, a lot of the torching was the rioters attacking Jewish merchants on the main drags.

I didn't go home during those few days. No one did. Everyone stayed at the paper 'til twelve, one o'clock, then got a little sleep and started again at eight. Everyone would go up on top of the *Free Press* building and you could see the city on fire. Detroit has this old street plan, it's designed by L'Enfant, the same guy who designed Washington, D.C., and you've got this downtown on the river and these spokes radiating out, so you could look up almost every street and you could see all the streets on fire. Every main street, every night, was ablaze. My wife and I got engaged the one night of the riot I didn't go out, a few days after we'd met. I remember sitting on a park bench in Lafayette Park and we decided to get married. You could sit there on that bench and see the town on fire.

Sometime during that week I wrote a short piece on this one kid that was killed, a hillbilly kid. I just took the police stuff and they said he was seen carrying a weapon, a shotgun, and that he was coming down the stairs with this long weapon and the national guard yelled at him to stop and he didn't so they killed him. It was just like every other story: every death was always the fault of the people who were killed.

Then, about ten days after it was all over, one day I was sitting at my desk and a guy came off the elevator with two kids about eight and nine years old and he said, "I'm looking for Mr. Serrin." You couldn't do that today, with all the guards and everything they have at newspapers but then people could just walk in off the street. And he was very stern, not angry, but stern. And he said, "Mr. Serrin, you wrote the story on my son." And it was the father of the hillbilly kid. And I said, "Yes, I did." And he said, "Well, I want you to know my son was not a sniper." And he showed me all these pictures of the young man laid out in an open casket in the house —maybe they were too poor for a funeral parlor—picture after picture. Each picture was different, with more nieces and nephews standing with their hands crossed, in front of the casket. And the father would say to me, "Does he look like a sniper? My son was not a sniper." He had driven with the two kids all the way from Tennessee to Detroit and parked his car and walked into the *Detroit Free Press* to tell me this. I took his name and number and said, "Thank you for coming here, let me look into this."

So I went out and talked to people and I found out that his son was one of these kids who had come to Detroit for decades to make some money and he was living in this apartment and working in some plant. People said he was a great kid. And then some people told me he had a broom that night he was killed. He was on the stairs with the broom and this guy just killed him, shot him dead.

Kurt Luedtke, who'd been editing the riot coverage, had gone up north and I called him up and I said, "We've really got to investigate every one of these deaths because they're bullshit." And I went to the city editor, Neal Shine, and told him the same thing. So Luedtke came back and we created this team, me, Barbara Stanton, and Gene Goltz, who had won a Pulitzer Prize in Texas for putting some sheriff in the slammer. So we began that investigation. We split up the forty-three people and we spent about a month interviewing people, getting police reports, and going back to where the shootings had occurred.

I remember this one case where these guys were drilled in a car. The police report said "shot while leaving the scene" and something like "three rounds fired." We found the car still parked and counted all the holes and there were maybe twenty holes in this car, and all this blood all over the joint. And we got some good cop stuff from some old-time police reporters and then we made friends with the coroner—one time Goltz gave him a fifth of whiskey, to show "our respect," Goltz said—and we looked at autopsy reports and we personally went and looked at a ton of those bodies.

We became convinced that almost every one of those deaths was bullshit. Like one guy was deaf and never even heard the police. And the hillbilly kid. And the Algiers Motel, where three people were executed. When the story ran there was a big, big to-do. The story was picked up across the country, and there was not a single retraction or correction on any of that stuff. And it was all because of that father coming up.

I think the story did make for some changes, that plus the weight of other riot coverage. And just the times were changing. The cops came under intense scrutiny for the next several years and they began slowly to make an effort to hire black policemen. And the authorities set up a committee which had an effect for awhile and white people became sensitive to black people.

I was changed, too. I mean I obviously had changed in Korea, and I had seen some things there that had opened my eyes to how the world worked, and even before the riot I wrote a lot of iconoclastic stuff. But the riot sort of changed my life. I really began to distrust cops and other authorities and I had not had that experience before in journalism. Before the riot a lot of my goals were things like to rise in journalism, go to Vietnam and cover that as a journalist. Afterward, I threw aside the sort of goofy ambitious things and just decided I wanted to be a more responsible, very basic journalist. The story was right here, not in Washington or Paris or Vietnam, but right here. So I became sort of an urban affairs writer and I did a lot of looking at the police department and stuff like that.

Eventually I left the *Free Press*. I knew I probably wasn't going to go anywhere there because a lot of people had come to distrust me. From their point of view my reporting was too one-sided and certainly anti-establishment. They thought I was too radical but I thought I was just a hard, tough journalist.

The town continued to empty out; in the '50 census it was over two million and now it's probably less than half that. The downtown is gone.

When Judy and I got married we made a commitment to the city and moved into Detroit, but finally, in 1979, we left.

Detroit is dead now. All the theaters are gone and then they built the Ren Center and that didn't work and they put a hotel across from it and that's not working. The new downtown is now out in the suburban ring. I went to Detroit for the first time when I was about fifteen years old, and I mean, it was like going to New York or Paris. Now Detroit's over. It's over.

PART

V

THE SEVENTIES

□

15

GENE MILLER
Back from Death Row

IN NOMINATING GENE MILLER OF THE *MIAMI HERALD* FOR his second Pulitzer Prize in 1976, in recognition of his successful efforts to obtain the freedom of two men wrongly convicted of first-degree murder and sentenced to the electric chair, John Knight, editorial chairman of the Knight-Ridder papers, wrote: "That justice was at last delivered to Freddie Pitts and Wilbert Lee is a milestone of American journalism. It is a reassertion of how essential that frail reed of a free press is to our society."

Over the course of the more than eight years it took to free Pitts and Lee, two black men who had been accused of murdering two white men in 1963, Miller and the paper were swept up in a system of justice that retained a powerful resemblance to the old South. Miller came to believe Pitts' and Lee's contentions that they had been beaten before their confessions. He also witnessed a trial in which the two men were tried before a judge who refused to allow an all-white jury to hear the taped confession of another man that he had actually committed the crime. In all, the *Herald* ran more than two-hundred stories on the case, continuing to pour money and time into the effort despite the fact that the incidents relating to the case all transpired six-hundred miles from Miami in the Florida panhandle, where the paper did not even circulate.

For Miller, whose work on two other cases of miscarriage of justice had led to an earlier Pulitzer, the Pitts-Lee case was a long and often discouraging one, made harder by the fact that he was repeatedly villified as an outside agitator. But according to Miller, perhaps the hardest thing for him to deal with was his belief that he was obliged, based on the facts of the case, to shed his reporter's "objective" stance and become an advocate—recruiting lawyers, amassing evidence, and helping to prepare a series of legal challenges—while eventually removing himself from day-to-day reporting on the case.

It's virtually impossible to discern what motivated Miller, now an editor at the *Herald,* since he hides his feelings beneath a joking, self-mocking manner. Born in 1928, he grew up in the Midwest as a middle-class, church-going, boy scout. He says that "If I had any sense I'd be back in Indiana running the family electroplating business." He describes himself as a workaholic, candidly admitting that part of the price of winning his Pulitzers was spending very little time with his four children. "Years later they told me how much they resented my working so much," he says.

Was it race or the system that was at fault in the Pitts-Lee case? "Both," says Miller. "The system can misfire at any level." He adds, "If you ascertain how many people are in jail on first-degree murder charges in America, and if you assume that the system doesn't work one percent of the time, there's going to be a lot more cases."

Following is a portion of the last story Miller wrote about the Pitts-Lee case.

THE MIAMI HERALD
September 20, 1975

PITTS, LEE WALK AS FREE MEN
by
GENE MILLER

FLORIDA STATE PRISON—Freddie Lee Pitts and Wilbert Lee walked away from the shadow of death at 37 minutes after noon Friday. They did not look back.

The clamorous din of men behind bars faded behind them. A wave of men behind cameras receded before them.

Unsmiling, Pitts and Lee acknowledged neither.

After 12 years and 48 days imprisonment for another man's crime, they walked into the world, free men, a Xerox copy of the governor's pardon folded in their billfolds.

"I've had enough of this hotel," Pitts said mildly. "They have very poor accommodations."

"I've got my prison clothes off and I've got my free world clothes on," said Lee, "and gee, baby, I feel like a Philadelphia lawyer."

Their lawyers, Irwin J. Block and Phillip A. Hubbart, drove them to Gainesville where they boarded a Boeing 727 to Miami.

Lee was apprehensive. It was his first time in the air.

"For nine years I was facing the electric chair," he said. "I guess I can face the airplane."

He did. At 29,000 feet he grinned, "The spirit's got me."

GENE MILLER:
THE STORY BEHIND THE STORY

As a lifer at the *Herald,* I was a general assignment reporter for years prior to parole as an editor in 1984. I never considered myself an investigative reporter. The criminal justice system always intrigued me, and through Warren Holmes, a polygraph man with a low opinion of the polygraph, I heard about the three murder cases that led to the Pulitzers.

In the Pitts-Lee case, Warren, an ex-cop with a ruthlessly logical mind, tested an innocent woman accused of a murder. Her boyfriend, she said, committed that crime—and he had killed two other gas station attendants in Port St. Joe, Florida, four years before. Two black men, Freddie Pitts and Wilbert Lee, were on Death Row for the gas station homicides. She didn't even know their names. Then Holmes interrogated the boyfriend and broke him. He admitted everything and that's where the story began.

I went to the Florida Panhandle and worked seven weeks on the first piece. Police had beaten a confession out of the two black men and their own lawyer had persuaded them to repeat it in the courtroom in an attempt to save their lives. I knew it wasn't going to be easy to get white people to change their minds about guilt.

I worked the case for eight years whenever I could. We managed to come up with a couple of superb lawyers who did everything pro bono, and that was important. I became totally obsessed. I'd get up at two o'clock in the morning and sit on the front step and make notes. I just couldn't stop thinking about it. I made the mental commitment to do everything I could to correct a severe malfunction of justice. I stayed in Holiday Inns so often that I came to detest them. Even today I can't stand them.

There aren't any secrets to what I did. It was just a lot of hard work, running down absolutely everything, checking and checking again. I'm very thorough and I'm very persistent.

The low point came when Pitts and Lee finally got a new trial and an all-white jury in the Panhandle convicted them a second time. I saw it coming. The judge wouldn't let the jury hear the taped confession from the real killer—and he wouldn't testify without immunity. Along the way, I got slugged coming out of the courthouse with a fifty or sixty-pound file on my shoulder. A relative of one of the murdered men didn't like me. I'd never met him.

When the governor and the Florida cabinet finally pardoned Pitts and Lee, I walked out of the prison with them and wrote a final story, the release story. I told them at the time I felt great happiness—but that I would never write about them again as long as I lived. And I haven't. Part of the reason was to allow them to get along with their lives. They've done well. And part of the reason was to get along with my life. I have.

There's a line between reporting and advocacy and obviously I crossed it, and I was quite uncomfortable. I didn't like it at all. I dislike opinion pieces. In Pitts-Lee, though, I had a bear by the tail and couldn't let go. There is enormous diversity of opinion on most cases, most episodes, most events. And as journalists we feel compelled to give two sides or five sides or ten sides. But sometimes only one side is right and the other nine are wrong. We don't often make that judgment. In the Pitts-Lee case, I had to.

16

STANLEY FORMAN

Capturing Drama Through the Photographer's Lens

STANLEY FORMAN IS SITTING IN THE LIVING ROOM OF HIS house on Cape Cod, supposedly taking it easy after an operation. But as he talks, his words tumbling out almost faster than he can form them, he looks as though he's ready to spring out of his chair and grab his camera at the first sign of action.

Forman, who won Pulitzer Prizes for spot news photography in 1976 and 1977, and who was part of a winning staff effort for feature photography in 1979, is, by his own description, a life-long news hound. "I love news," he says. "I've had a police radio in my bedroom since I was eight or nine years old."

Born in 1945, Forman has always lived in the Boston area, a fact readily apparent from his accent and his command of Boston city geography. His first and only paper was the Hearst-owned *Boston Record American,* later renamed the *Boston Herald American* after Hearst bought a competing publication and merged the papers. Ten years later, when it looked as though the successor paper might die (Rupert Murdoch eventually bought it) Forman switched over to become a video cameraman at a local television station.

But he still misses newspaper work, Forman says, even though as a recent father he claims to have slowed down a bit from his fire-chasing days. "If I did have the chance to go back to stills, would I?" he muses. "I don't know if I'm hungry enough but I think I would. I used to be somebody in stills. In TV, if you're not in front of the camera you're almost nothing."

One of the series of photos for which Forman won his first Pulitzer, and the single photo for which he won his second, follow.

Stanley Forman was photographing a ladder rescue in Boston's Back Bay when a fire escape gave way. Forman won a 1976 Pulitzer Prize for his dramatic series of shots of the ensuing tragedy, in which a young woman fell to her death and her godchild was injured.

Stanley Forman won his second Pulitzer, in 1977,
for photographing the beating of a black lawyer
by white high school students in front of Boston's City Hall.

Stanley Forman/BostonHerald American

STANLEY FORMAN:
THE STORY BEHIND THE STORY

When I was a kid growing up in Revere I used to be a spark—a person who chases fires. I chased police cars, too. When I was young I used to go with my father and later I used to go with friends. My dad was a musician —he played accordion and had his own band—but he just liked to go to these things.

I was planning on becoming a policeman or a fireman but when I was about eighteen or nineteen, already out of high school, my father got me a camera and said, "You go to all these things; why don't you start taking pictures?" I took a year's photography course at Franklin Institute in Boston and then I got my first job in 1966 working as campaign photographer for the state attorney-general, Edward Brooke, in his first campaign for the United States Senate. The people in his campaign inter-viewed everybody at Franklin Institute and I'm sure what enthused them about me was what I told them about how I had a darkroom and how I got up in the middle of the night and went to things and kept crazy hours. They knew the job was going to involve long hours and it did.

But it was a wonderful experience. If you shook Brooke's hand, I took your picture. I had someone with me who took down the name and address. I would make three prints of each picture: one for the person, one for the file and one for the local newspaper. I just shot and shot—as many pictures as I could get.

At the end of the campaign, the public relations man, Jerry Sadow, called the three Boston newspapers and got me interviews at all three. The *Herald* offered me a job as a custodian and said maybe I could work myself up to the photo department; the *Globe* had no interest whatsoever; and the *Record-American*'s chief photographer, Myer Ostroff, hired me as a trainee. I was supposed to scrub the sinks and mix the chemicals and when someone didn't want to do a print I would do that—basically I was like a gofer.

My real start as a news photographer came about a month after I began at the paper. I had gone to a Boston Bruins hockey game and when I came home I had the fire radio on. I heard that a train had crashed into a gasoline truck on the Everett-Chelsea line. I got there and I was the first photographer there. I shot the one roll of film I had—I didn't have extra film, I didn't have enough flash bulbs—and I made some fantastic pictures. Somewhere around twelve people died and I had eight of the victims, I mean not gruesome pictures, newsworthy pictures. The next day I owned the paper.

The *Record-American* was a wonderful place to work for someone who didn't have a family, didn't need a lot of money, and just wanted to be a news photographer. We kicked ass. I learned from the fellows from the roaring '20s. If somebody tragically died and we needed to talk to the family, we knew how to knock on doors. A lot of times now I'll say to a reporter, "We've got to knock on that door." And they say, "Why?" and I say, "Because we have to show a picture of that kid who was in the accident," or whatever. I mean, I'll do it myself. It's important. You don't identify with somebody unless you see them.

At the *Record-American* and at the *Herald* photographers and reporters worked hand in hand. If there was a good murder story, the team went out. If there was a hurricane, the team went out. We rode in one car. I got along with almost all of the reporters, and most of them were fun. There were a few that were selfish, though. I remember one guy I cruised with for a long time who, if it wasn't a good word story, couldn't have cared less about my pictures. And I cared about his word story all the time. The managing editors and editors, as far as I was concerned, never thought as much of photographers as they thought about reporters.

You don't see newspaper photographers and reporters working together as much as you used to, at least in the Boston area. A lot of things have changed since then. I think there's an awful lot of emphasis on presentation today. I watch some of these photographers and sometimes I think some of them don't even know how to run from one corner to the other. Everything is so slow and meticulous. When's the last time you saw a great spot news picture? Since 1983, which is when I went into TV, I can only name maybe four or five pictures in the Boston area where I've seen them and said, "Boy, I wish I had been there for that." I think maybe TV is partly to blame—you turn on the TV and you see these people live, crying on TV after a hurricane; it's pretty tough to beat that. News pictures have become kind of passé. But there's also the fact that everything's become so much more sophisticated—the cameras, the film, the developer—and newspapers have spent a lot of money on engraving and other things to get good print quality.

When I began, you didn't need to be a great technician—you'd come back, slap the negative in, and print it. I'm not a great technician myself although I enjoy things like thinking about the depth of field, getting the exposure right, working out the amount of available light at night and all that. What I did have were great news instincts. The big thing in being a news photographer is you anticipate. You remember the days of Bob Cousy of the Celtics? I mean, he just knew when to go to the left, when to go to the right. I'm not as good as Bob Cousy but I have the instincts. You just know, you anticipate, the peak of the action, you know what's coming next, you're always thinking. You don't just go in there and flub around. You're also thinking, "How soon are they going to throw me out of the area? How much time do I have?" All these things are part of the instincts of this game, this news game.

And you've got to want to work. When I was working for a newspaper I was never really off. When I was single I'd go out on a Friday night, drop off my date, and go cruising. Or on a Saturday night, after I got off work, I'd stay out 'til sunrise, just cruising around, drinking coffee, reading the papers, going from one call to another. Even if I was covering a story I was tuned in to what else might be going on. I had scanners for police and fire calls everywhere—still do: in the car, in the house. I've had a scanner in my bedroom since I was probably eight or nine years old. My wife Debbie always says, "Turn it down," but then she goes to sleep and she doesn't hear it in the middle of the night. I always feel that I want to have the radio on so that if I miss something, it's because I blew it myself. I said recently to Debbie, "You know, we don't have any music in this house, we just have scanners." And she said, "That's your music."

One thing you never get over is worrying whether your pictures came out. I hear some of these photographers say, "Oh, I got great stuff." You don't have great stuff until you see that image, I don't care who you are. I always say, "I *might* have some good stuff if it comes out." I still remember one night hearing on the radio that there was a jumper in front of the children's hospital by the Harvard Medical School. When I got there, there was this young girl going to jump—not from very high up, probably no more than fifteen feet—and the fire department came and they had a blanket out for her. I was taking all kinds of pictures but without the flash, because I've always felt at a suicide scene that if they're going to jump they're not going to jump because my flash went off.

After about an hour and a half they put a ladder up and they went up to get her and she jumped into the net. Bang! I put the flash on because I knew it was happening and I got her midair, arms flailing. I went back to the office and developed the film and it wasn't there; the flash didn't go off when she was in mid-air, didn't recycle fast enough. I was sick waiting for the papers to come out. But you know what? There were two other cameramen there and they didn't get it either.

I started at the paper in 1966 and by the middle of 1975 I was getting bored. I was sort of in a slump and I was having trouble even making features. So on my birthday, July 10, I took the exam for the fire department. Twelve days later, I was working 10 a.m. to 6 p.m. and around four o' clock I was trying to figure out how to take an early slide. As I walked by the assignment desk they struck a box—the fire department put out an alarm—and the first call I heard was Engine 33 and Ladder 17. Within thirty seconds a box came in and instead of an engine and a ladder they were sending three engines and two ladders and a chief. They were talking about people trapped in a building.

Well, I ran out of the newsroom. I didn't even know exactly where it was but I knew it was the Back Bay because the box was a 1500 area box. I went up Harrison Avenue toward the South End and there's a fire station there, Engine 3, and Engine 3 was just going out on the box and I got behind them. We got to Boylston Street and of course Engine 3 went through the red light and there was a damn mailtruck that wouldn't let me go through but I finally got around him. The fire was on Marlborough Street, Dartmouth and Marlborough. I parked the car and they were still screaming, "Get a ladder truck to the rear of the building," "Ladder truck to the rear of the building," so I ran down to Marlborough and I saw there was heavy, heavy smoke pouring out the windows.

I ran around to the back of the building and when I got there a firefighter was just climbing off the roof onto the back fire escape and below him a woman and a child were huddled next to the window, just ducking down. They moved the engine company that was there out of the way and the ladder truck came down the alley and parked and I got some pictures of the firefighter up there. I climbed up onto the bed of the truck where the ladder rests so I'd have a little more height and a little better angle. I had my motor drive on, set for three frames a second. As far as I was concerned it was just going to be another good ladder rescue picture. The ladder was going up and the firefighter who'd come down from the roof was guiding it toward the fire escape. He was going to climb onto the ladder, the woman would hand him the baby, he would hand the baby to a firefighter coming up from the bottom, then he would help her onto the ladder and they'd be out of there. Routine ladder rescue.

And then the fire escape let go. I just kept shooting as they came down. At the end I said to myself, "I don't want to see them hit," and I turned around. As it worked out the woman and the baby fell behind a fenced area. I couldn't have seen them hit anyway. When I finally turned around again people were screaming and yelling and there was the fireman who'd been on the fire escape, hanging onto the ladder by one arm, like a monkey. He had all his gear on but he managed to hoist himself back up onto the ladder.

I came back off the ladder truck and of course I was shaking. The little baby had already gone in the ambulance and the woman, who was the baby's godmother, was still on the ground and they were trying to revive her. I was going to switch lenses but I couldn't find my 20 mm lens and all of a sudden I started thinking, "Oh my God, I lost a lens, I'm going to be in the shit now"—these are the things going through your head. Then I decided I better get out of there. I always have this fear that a well-meaning relative is going to rip the camera off my neck so I always run as soon as I've got my pictures. So I was running out the alley and there was the firefighter who's been on the fire escape. I went up to him and I said, "Nice job"—I didn't know what to say—and he was looking at me, dazed, and he kept saying, "Two more seconds I would have had them, two more seconds."

I raced back to the office and I walked into the office of my boss, Myer Ostroff, and I told him what I had and I said, "If these pictures don't come out I won't be into work tomorrow and I might never come back." I developed the film and he looked at the negatives and he saw that I was a nervous wreck and he said, "Stanley, do me a favor, just go over there and sit back." Meyer wrote a note to the publisher who was in the middle of a meeting and he came in and he looked at the pictures and he said, "Did anybody else get this?" And my only response was, "I don't know but they didn't get anything better than I did."

Later I went home and about eight o'clock that night Dennis Brearley, a photographer, called me to tell me that the baby was alright but that the woman died. And I said, "Do you think they're still going to run the pictures?" I really said that. I have to be honest with you. I did say that. And he said, "Oh sure." That night there was a fire in the North End and my neighbor called me and we went out about two o'clock but it was nothing. Afterward we stopped in a store to see the paper and I said, "Oh, Wow!" I couldn't believe it. I had the whole front page plus all of page three.

The next day my boss called me into his office and said, "You have some great pictures and you're going to win a lot of awards but I don't want you to be disappointed if you don't win a Pulitzer because of the problems between Pulitzer and Hearst." We were a Hearst paper and that's how they thought, even though I don't think by then it made any difference. My own geography didn't go beyond Boston. I mean, I knew what the Pulitzer was, but whoever thought of winning it? I worked for sixteen years at the *Herald* and I know they had only entered once before my year. The only thing I could think that day while my pictures were being developed was that I was going to win spot news in the Boston Press Photographers Association contest.

So the year went by and there was legislation passed about fire escapes. I put together a presentation for the Pulitzer and I remember the publisher said to me, "Stanley, if you win the Pulitzer I'm going to fly you and your family down wherever they have the awards." I had done my research and I knew that at that time there wasn't any award ceremony so I said, "Well, we can have the party in the mailroom then." And he said, "What do you mean?" And I said, "They mail it to you."

My presentation must have been at least two inches thick, and it was heavy: 16 × 20 pictures and a dozen clips from around the world—I had 129 different newspaper clips that people sent me—all matted down and everything. I decided to deliver it in person so I drove down with a friend, Al LaPorte. When we got there I left him in the car and I went upstairs and I presented this thing and they gave me a receipt and they said, "Mr. Hohenberg would certainly like to meet you." So I went in and Mr. Hohenberg, who was in charge, started telling me about the year before, about how the winner, Gerald Gay, had a presentation that was just wonderful, so simple, just a board with the picture on it. Well, I left there with my heart in my toes. I went back heartbroken, thinking I'd really lost it.

When the winners of all the photo contests for the year started being announced it turned out that I had won everything. I was in Amsterdam to get the prize for winning the World Press photo contest when I heard I'd won the Pulitzer. I got a telegram saying, "You won the big one." I was in Amsterdam for what everybody else thought was the big one 'but in American journalism, the big one is the Pulitzer.

But before I knew I'd won the first Pulitzer I'd already taken the picture that won the following year, so I didn't really get to enjoy the first one because I was already worrying about the second one. I took that one in April. I was in the office one day and I went up to the assistant city editor, Al Salie, and I said, "What's doing?" and he said, "There's an antibusing thing down at City Hall," and he said one of the other photographers was there. And I said, "Can I go down there and help out?" — Not thinking there would be any trouble, just wanting to get out of the office. There was a protest practically every day at that time. There was periodic violence and protests and you know, it was spring and these kids were skipping school to come down to City Hall.

So I went down there and I parked and I sauntered in and as I was walking up the steps to the council chambers where the group was, they were coming down. So I was in front of them and all the other photographers were behind them or in the middle. It's like hitting Megabucks; if it's your day, it's your day. As they came out onto the plaza there was a group of blacks about to go in to tour city hall. There was a little scuffle right on the steps so I switched to a wide angle lens to get it all in. Then they started walking down toward the old state house and I happened to look up and I saw this black man taking the corner and I thought, "My God, they're going to beat him up."

It was like the gauntlet, everybody started taking a punch. I could hear that the camera wasn't transporting the film right so I started shooting single frame, and of course I had this super wide-angle lens on so I had to be within a few feet of what was going on to get a big enough image of the action. There was another black guy who happened to stroll by and he just got himself out of the way. But the first guy was just caught. One of the high school kids happened to have a flag in his hand, I guess because the group had had a flag with them, so he used it as a weapon. There was no significance to that fact, but there was no thought of "Let's not do it with the flag" either. Then the cops moved in and it was all over.

So that was the second Pulitzer. It didn't get as much play as it should have because that same day Howard Hughes died. The top of the paper was "Howard Hughes Dead" and my picture was below the fold. After I won the second Pulitzer I entered some other pictures I thought were good but they didn't even get into the finals. The whole photo staff won for the coverage of the blizzard of '78. Although I have a sixteenth of that award I was out injured and I didn't do much on that. And then I went into television.

Since I won, Boston has gone Pulitzer crazy. If I could show you some of the entries, it's embarrassing. But of course that's easy for me to say because I've won all the awards.

17

JOE HUGHES
Plane Crash Over San Diego

WHEN A PACIFIC SOUTHWEST AIRLINES BOEING 727 COLLIDED with a small plane over San Diego on a September morning in 1978, only twenty-eight minutes remained before the San Diego *Evening Tribune*'s presses were scheduled to roll. The paper threw virtually its entire staff into the effort and, by extending the deadline forty minutes, managed to produce a first edition that included a page one aerial photograph of the crash site—a six-square-block area in an older neighborhood of the city—plus half a dozen stories and additional photographs. Two more editions followed in rapid order, each one containing additional details on the crash, which killed 144 people.

Joe Hughes was one of the *Tribune* reporters immediately dispatched to the scene. A San Diego native and self-effacing veteran reporter, Hughes, who was born in 1942, already had a reputation for speed and coolness under fire—one of his earlier exploits having consisted of catching film thrown by a photographer who was pinned down during a shootout and then racing back to the paper to get it developed. To hear Hughes tell it, he haplessly stumbled his way through the day, picking up scraps of information while trying to avoid any direct confrontation with the crash's gory results. In fact, Hughes not only contributed information to the rewrite man putting together successive versions of the lead story but also dictated a moving piece from the scene, part of which is included here.

Revisiting the scene of the crash ten years later, Hughes searches carefully, but for the most part in vain, for traces of the tragedy. Houses have been rebuilt, streets have been repaved, and the city sits quietly under the southern California sun.

THE EVENING TRIBUNE
September 25, 1978

DEVASTATING BOOM OF TRAGEDY SHATTERS A QUIET NEIGHBORHOOD
by
JOE HUGHES

It was shortly after 9 a.m. and North Park, a community of mostly small, old houses and elderly, retired persons, was quietly heading into another hot and clear September morning.

Mary Costa was finishing breakfast and settling down to watch a morning television show in her home at 3575 Boundary St.

Outside her door and around the corner, Jim Garton, skateboard under his arm, was heading for a nearby bus stop and a day at the beach. . . .

The temperature gauge on the California Bank tower building on University Avenue already was creeping past the 80 mark.

And the clock showed 9:02.

At precisely that moment, North Park went from calm to catastrophe.

A Pacific Southwest Airlines jetliner and a small Cessna had collided in midair in a loud, thunderous explosion.

"I thought it was a loud sonic boom," said Mary Costa. "But it seemed too loud and too close. I opened the shades and looked up. All I could see was black smoke and pieces of things falling from the sky.

"I knew something terrible had happened. I rushed next door to where a little lady friend lived all alone. But her house was all smoke and flames.

"Then I panicked and started to run away from it all; I didn't know what to do.". . .

At the corner of Nile and Dwight, onlookers stood at the curb in stunned silence as rescue crews started arriving on the scene. It was 9:30 a.m.

JOE HUGHES:
THE STORY BEHIND THE STORY

I was in the city room, talking on the phone to a friend of mine who's a construction superintendent, and I could hear someone saying in the background that a PSA plane had crashed in North Park. Then you could hear the chatter on the police radio in the city room. I told my friend what I'd heard and he looked out of his construction trailer and he could see the plume of black smoke. So he hung up and I hung up and I was told to go out to the scene. At the time I was doing what we call enterprise reporting—general features, investigations—but in this case they just cleared the city room. There were no specifics, just "Go out to the scene." There was no particular buzz in the newsroom that I remember but we could tell it sounded heavy.

My wife at the time was a stewardess for PSA but I really didn't think at the time that she might be on the flight. PSA is a commuter airline, up and down all day long, and I didn't usually pay that much attention to her schedule.

I didn't know what streets were closed and what ones were open, so I drove to a little park a couple miles from the scene of the crash and parked there. While I was driving, there were a lot of sirens and police cars going by. It was one of the hottest days of the year, what we call a Santa Ana condition, when the searing heat from the desert blows in and combines with the ocean airflow. After I'd parked I ran to the scene, stopping to talk to a few people who I thought might have seen something. I remember I talked to a milkman and a few other people but they hadn't seen much.

Finally I got close enough to where I could see the devastation. The police lines were already up but you could see it was like an A-bomb had hit. The plane had come down in the middle of an intersection and then it took two hops and broke up over a two- to three-block area. There was some debris spread around but most of it was fairly concentrated. Homes were burning up—some were completely destroyed but you couldn't tell it at that point because of the billowing black smoke from the fires. There was a piece of the tail of the plane in the middle of the street and I could see a PSA logo on it. Then I saw a piece of a stewardess's uniform that had probably been torn off her body hanging from the telephone wires and that's when it kind of hit home that at least some people had died. Just for a brief second I thought about my wife and what might have happened and then I kept interviewing people.

At one point I saw this lady who I recognized from the office as the secretary to one of the editors. Two police were holding onto her and she was crying and hysterical. It seems she was talking on the phone to her mother who lived right there where the plane went in and all of a sudden the line went dead. She was trying to get through and saying she was from the newspaper but there was no way she could get any closer anyway because of the fires.

At a lot of things like this you see people running to the scene and gawking but in this case, they'd go up, take a peek, and walk away. They didn't want to see any more. It was gory, no question about that. Some friends of mine saw pieces of bodies but I just didn't want to look that close.

Finally—I didn't have a watch on so I didn't even know what time it was—I decided I had enough for a story. I tried to find a phone to call the city desk and that's when I found out that the phones were all out. I decided it was too far to try to go back to the car so I started running the other way, knocking on doors, asking "Is your phone working?" I don't know how many miles I went, two or three maybe, sweating, soaking wet because it was so hot, trying to think what I was going to say when I finally got to a phone. Finally someone let me in and let me use their phone to call in and I dictated the story. It went in the paper just as I dictated it—I didn't write anything out. I also talked to Jim Nichols, the rewrite man who was putting together the main story for each edition. I don't know how he did it, he was just cool as a cucumber.

After that, I went back to the office to regroup. I got chewed out by the city editor because he said I shouldn't have come back, because in the meantime they were formulating the game plan and I was supposed to be a team leader. By this time the second edition had already gone and they were still formulating the game plan, so you can see things were happening pretty fast.

I called my wife and she was at home. I think I was really overdramatic; I said, "A lot of your friends are dead." And that was true, she knew everyone who was killed on the plane because she'd been working there about ten years.

I went back out all kinds of times, just to see the cleanup and everything. There was really no end to the story. It just kept rolling through the night and people just did their thing and when they were exhausted they left and people picked up and continued doing follow stories. So there was no going anywhere to drink or do anything or talk it over. It was just, go home and sleep.

To this day when friends of mine in the business get together the subject of the crash still comes up. Nobody's seen anything since that's been that bad.

PART

VI

THE EIGHTIES

◻

18

ALBERT SCARDINO
The Life and Death of a Weekly Newspaper

HE LOOKS AND SOUNDS LIKE A CROSS BETWEEN A GOOD OLD boy and a Harvard government professor. There's the slow Southern speech and boyish, unlined face that bring to mind images of warm nights and fancy cotillions. But there's also the dark socks and bow tie, and the long discourses on public policy, that tell of years spent beyond the confines of the old South.

Actually, it was Columbia, not Harvard, that provided Albert Scardino's introduction to life outside of Savannah, Georgia. From there, by a circuitous route, he returned in his late twenties to Savannah and founded the weekly *Georgia Gazette*, which he and his wife, Marjorie, ran for seven financially precarious years before finally abandoning the effort in 1985.

It was in the paper's waning days that Scardino won a Pulitzer Prize for a series of editorials written in 1983 that highlighted the paper's tough reporting on issues ranging from state government corruption to local misuse of tax-free bonds. The writing is strong and personal; here is someone who isn't afraid to say what he thinks, but who has the knack of delivering his opinions with style and grace.

For all of his memories of marching for civil rights while attending an all-white private high school, or standing on the roof of Carman Hall at Columbia University watching the cops bust heads in 1968, Scardino, who was born in 1948, does not come across as someone seared and moulded by the powerful events of his youth. He seems, rather, almost something out of the nineteenth century—the educated, decent-thinking small-town editor who is part and parcel of the life of his community. He believes in government, and in the ability of a newspaper to help shape public officials' actions to good ends.

If there is passion, it is reserved for his beloved paper. His eyes light up as he remembers how he used to make the rounds of the vending machines on Sunday morning with the oldest of his three children to make sure they were all in working order. And there's a certain relish in his voice as he recalls walking into some of the town's fancier restaurants only to have other patrons get up and leave.

Scardino went back to being a reporter for several years after the *Gazette* folded, writing for the *New York Times* while he and his wife continued to pay off their leftover debts. Later, he became press secretary to David Dinkins, New York City's first African-American mayor.

Following is one of the editorials for which Scardino won a Pulitzer Prize.

GEORGIA GAZETTE
June 22–28, 1983

THE CALDWELL REPORT

The citizens of Georgia owe a debt to the members of the state Campaign and Financial Disclosure Commission for the thorough and patient analysis they compiled over the past ten months of Sam Caldwell's illegal activities.

When the investigation started last summer, Caldwell and his cronies in the state Dept. of Labor snickered at the commission. Few citizens had ever heard of the panel, and the professional politicians of Georgia had nothing but contempt for what they called the "niggling" forms which had to be filed with the commission each election year.

The arrogance of the politicians reached dizzying proportions last winter when 19 state senators threatened to pass a law abolishing the commission if it didn't leave poor old Sam alone. We're proud to say that the members of this obscure agency had the courage to perform their duty to the citizens of the state rather than succumb to the threat. At the same time, we're embarrassed that two senators from Chatham County, Tom Coleman and Al Scott, participated in that effort to intimidate the commission.

Caldwell has disgraced himself, his friends, his supporters and his state. When he finally leaves office, we'll probably find a ring around the labor department building in Atlanta. Thanks to the work of the elections commission, we have let the professional politicians and their hangers-on know that the rules have not changed. The government still belongs to the people.

ALBERT SCARDINO:
THE STORY BEHIND THE STORY

When I was growing up, the racial situation in Savannah was so blatant that it was not difficult to tell right from wrong. You encountered it when you took the maid home. You knew she got $18 a week and when you dropped her off, you could see that it was a dirt street with forty shanties on either side of the street and an outhouse at the end of the block. Or when you walked through the Sears store and there were two water fountains and one said "whites only" it just didn't make any sense.

My father, who is a urologist, came to Savannah from Houston. I had six brothers and sisters. I had an older brother and sister who at the same time that I was becoming aware of issues like civil rights were going through the social and sexual revolution. We'd all sit around the dinner table all the time and talk about politics. There was an enormous premium on expression in our house. The one way of getting attention was to have something to say.

There was a group of traditional Southern liberals in Savannah who got together and decided that Savannah was not going to become the same kind of racial battleground as Selma had and they put pressure on the business community to integrate the restaurants and theaters and hotels. My father was one of the people participating in that so I always assumed that that was a reasonable way to behave.

I got into journalism in kind of an accidental way. Somebody had to be the editor of the school paper in my senior year and nobody had exhibited a whole lot of interest. The editor that year asked me if I would do it. I went to a training program at Northwestern for the summer, and when I went back I decided not to edit the newspaper after all but to edit the yearbook, because the editor of the newspaper had to answer to a faculty committee and the editor of the yearbook didn't.

But I stayed interested in journalism. The summer after I graduated from high school my brother-in-law, who'd bought a small weekly newspaper in Atlanta, asked me to come and work for him for $20 a week. I went up and started sweeping and doing classified ads and he asked me if I wanted to write anything. So I started a political column. It was the summer that Jimmy Carter was running for governor for the first time. So I went flying around interviewing all the politicians and being taken very seriously because they didn't have any idea who I was writing for. By the time they realized it, the summer was over and I was off to college. Every summer after that I worked for a different newspaper.

For me, the attraction of journalism was always not so much the journalism itself as the opportunity to comment on and participate in the public process — to have something to say about public policy and to have an excuse to be involved. I never had an interest in composing for the sake of composing. For a long time I had ambitions to go to law school and get directly involved by running for public office. The purpose was the same: to have some ability to change the way people were using the arms of government.

After going to college at Columbia I spent six months working for the AP in West Virginia. That's where I met Marjorie. She was the slot editor. Eventually we both went to graduate school — Marjorie to finish her law degree and me to get a master's degree in journalism — and we got married in 1974. We came back to Georgia to do a film about the Georgia coast for PBS. In the process I got to know the area in a way I had always wanted to know it and after a year I really thought I had a firm grasp of most of the social and political and economic issues in the whole region.

In the meantime, Marjorie started practicing law as a way of getting food on the table and paying off student loans. She was in a small, very politically active law firm. Sometimes the lawyers all went out to lunch together and they would call me occasionally and take pity on me and invite me along. We'd talk about whatever was going on and two members of the firm in particular would say how the film had been really great but we don't need another movie, we need a decent newspaper. The *Savannah Morning News* and *Evening Press,* which were the same for all intents and purposes, were terrible newspapers. They were owned by a company that owned papers along the whole Savannah River Valley and most of the coast.

The lawyers in Marjorie's office said they'd raise the money for a new paper if I'd edit it. They said, "How much will it take to do a daily paper?" And I said, "$10 million." I had been through that community raising money for a $75,000 film and I knew there just wasn't $10 million of risk capital. And they said, "That can't be right—it can't take that much money." So we sat down and added up all the figures and we came up with $7 million. So they said, "How much would it take to start a weekly?" And we thought maybe we could do that for $100,000. So they said, "Okay, we'll raise the $100,000." They couldn't raise it, though.

We got ten people to put up $10,000 each. Marjorie and I were part of that. And then we got those same ten to put up another $50,000. And then at one point we did a stock offering. We ended up with about sixty-five investors, who put in as little as $50 and as much as $25,000. Over the life of the paper we raised a total of about $200,000 from investors. But it was a constant process of trying to get people to invest.

We started in April of 1978 and by the end of the summer we were out of money. The only salvation we could think of was to convince a free-distribution business paper that had been published for several years but was about to fold to merge with us so that we could qualify to be old enough to be the county's legal newspaper, which involves printing all the legal notices. At that time the daily paper had the contract. We agreed to give the free distribution paper $10,000 if we got the legal advertising and to split the profits with them for two years.

Then we went to the three officials who were responsible for granting the legal advertising contract, which was worth about $100,000 a year, and said, "We have a chance to buy this paper; would you give us a commitment to give us the legal advertising if we bought the paper?" And they said okay. The sheriff, who was the only Republican in town, was the first. He said that he just didn't think monopoly was a very good idea. This guy had been sheriff for sixteen or eighteen years. He thought Martin Luther King was a Communist. But something in his heart told him it was wrong for somebody to own the only newspaper in town. For awhile the legal advertising was about 40 percent of our revenue and it was all the profit.

But money wasn't the only problem. Marjorie, who was publisher of the paper, had just become a partner and she was doing a very good job with a corporate law practice, which of course meant her legal business was dependent on the corporate community. Later the paper caused the firm a lot of problems, especially when we got sued as often as we did and they were defending us, and some of the members thought it was wrecking the firm. So we were just tiptoeing into disaster.

At the beginning, we had about six months of goodwill. People thought the paper was cute. And it was. It was beautifully designed, which was not hard, especially when you were comparing it with a paper that was still going by '50s standards. I made up the paper from scratch. All you had to do was take the "Week in Review" section of the *Times* and three magazines and stand there with them open on the board and design the paper using bold rules and elegant typefaces.

And we thought about how would be the best way to do things. Savannah is a very old community with a real sense of history. So instead of calling the paper "Today in Savannah" or something like that we did some research and found out that the *Georgia Gazette* had been the first newspaper in the state and we took the masthead off and duplicated it. And we got somebody to do goldleaf lettering on the front window of our office and we sprinkled some dust around so it looked like we'd been there for a long time. And we put a little sign over the door which said, "Georgia's first newspaper."

There were so many things we were able to do that caught people's attention. There was no arts section in the daily paper so just putting together a calendar of events was revolutionary. Referring to people by their full name on first reference and everyone by last name only on second reference—doctors and preachers and women, even grandmothers —it was like a hurricane. We also had a theory that people buy newspapers more for the small print than for the front page. So we printed pages and pages of public record information—all the births and deaths and marriages and property transfers.

The business part didn't come so naturally, but fortunately Marjorie was involved with a lot of people who were very commercially oriented and they had a hell of a lot better sense than I did about how to do a project, how much money you needed to allocate to run an office, how much a photocopy machine should cost, and so on. Two or three of these guys went over budgets with me and we used the law firm's accountant. We got incorporated through the law firm's good graces and their office manager told us where to buy stationery. We had a friend who told us how to get a business license.

We went around and got to know three or four small printers and ended up buying some used typesetting equipment from them. Through them we met all the available typesetters in town. And we found somebody who was willing to serve as production manager and we hired a former salesperson from the daily paper as the advertising manager. We hired an experienced reporter who'd gone looking for work at the daily paper but had been told they didn't think the city was ready for a black street reporter so he'd have to work on the copy desk. He was one of our three reporters.

We hired a photographer who was probably the best news photographer in the state. But he was a drunk. The daily paper had given up on him three or four different times. I found different ways to keep him sober. He was also a magnificent reporter, despite being the most inarticulate son of a bitch you've ever encountered—you could barely understand him. Everybody would talk to him because they knew he couldn't write. But he would just absorb all this crap, and he would come back and sit down just before he passed out and tell everything that he had heard. Then he'd pass out and wake up maybe ten hours later and develop his photographs. Then he'd read what we'd written up and some of it would come back to him and he'd go off and start following the thread.

So we were an odd group, a bunch of people who just didn't fit into the neat slots everyone was used to. I decided that the only thing I could do to make sure everybody in town didn't take the paper as a joke—so that they didn't think this was some sort of alternative radical rag—was to wear a tie every day.

If your interest in life is sticking a stick in a beehive and stirring it up, running that paper was just the greatest joy that you could possible imagine. Pretty soon it became obvious to a large number of people that we were not going to abide by the standards of journalism that the daily paper had practiced for twenty-five years, and a lot of people didn't like it.

One story that made that clear was on the new courthouse. The clerk of the court was very unhappy about the new courthouse so I asked him what was wrong. He talked about not having enough shelf space for his records and how the county wanted him to microfilm everything and he didn't want to. He said, "But the real problem is there aren't enough bathrooms." I went back and looked at the architect's plans and then I said, "You say there aren't enough bathrooms but there are two bathrooms just at your end of the hall on your floor. Is that not enough?" And he said, "No, that's not enough; we need four." and I said, "Why?" He said, "Well, I'm not going to let any of these big nigger women come in and sit down on these toilets and I've got all these white girls working in my office." And I went back and wrote this up fairly straightforwardly. And made an enemy for a long, long time.

One of the most satisfying things about running the paper was that you could really see that what you wrote made a difference. There was a grade school principal who had gotten it in her mind that the children in her school were ruining their health by eating too much candy. I think she was a well-meaning person who had slipped a gear. She began conducting searches throughout the school and having female teachers do body searches of the girls for candy. It was easy to write a story about how ironic it was that fourth-graders, as part of their curriculum, had to memorize the Bill of Rights while in that same fourth grade they were experiencing this violation of the Fourth Amendment prohibition against unreasonable searches, and then to see within twenty-four hours the principal being suspended.

The biggest story we did involved the state labor commissioner, Sam Caldwell. He was the most powerful political figure in the state. There was an employee of the labor department who had been extorted for a campaign contribution and he went to the FBI and found out that the FBI was investigating a lot of other practices. He got all of his material together and took it to the *Atlanta Constitution* and waited six weeks and nothing appeared so he took it to the *Savannah Morning News* and he waited six more weeks and nothing appeared. Then he came to me and said, "You guys have a reputation for printing anything; would you print a story about Caldwell and what he's been doing?" And I said, "Sure, if it's true."

We ran the Caldwell story for six weeks as our lead story before anybody picked up on it. It turned out that Caldwell was involved not just in election fraud but in insurance fraud, real estate fraud, gambling, prostitution—he'd turned his department into a racketeering operation. In the end, almost forty people pleaded guilty or were convicted of felonies.

Some of the editorials I wrote about the Caldwell situation were among the ones that won the Pulitzer in 1984. We'd submitted things before but more to boost staff morale than for any other reason. Winning the Pulitzer was sort of a confirmation that yeah, that's what we started out to do. It was almost as if you'd been working in this vacuum for six or seven years not having any idea whether what you were doing was right or wrong.

But even the Caldwell stories didn't do much for our circulation. Our peak circulation was just over 4000; the daily paper had 30,000. I guess the people in town who were prepared to believe that the things we were writing about were going on already subscribed and read the paper. After we'd been operating for quite awhile I decided we should have charged more for the paper, say a dollar, instead of whatever it was—ten or fifteen cents we started out with—because the only people who were going to be interested in the paper were people who were interested in the public process, and for them it was a "must" buy.

If we'd charged more for the paper we also wouldn't have been as dependent on advertising. In thinking about it in retrospect I see that there are two big constitutional issues here. One is freedom of expression —it was a newspaper expressing a different point of view. And the other was freedom of commerce. It wasn't as though anyone who didn't like what we were writing said, "We'll get an injunction or a gag order." It was just, "We'll make damn sure whatever contracts you have get canceled and all the advertising you have will dry up."

We got to the point after about a year and a half or so where we'd have long, long discussions as the paper should have been going to press about what effect something was going to have on the finances. But we never figured out where to draw the line. Eventually we reached the conclusion that it really is not the responsibility of newspapers to be concerned with consequences. The minute you start considering the consequences of a story you begin compromising whatever it was you had to say.

That became the philosophy. We didn't have any idea whether it was worth it or not, until four years later, after we'd had the legal advertising for two years and then lost it back to the daily paper. We finally went back to the officials who have the say as to who gets the contract and asked them to change to us again. The clerk—the fellow I'd written about in the story on the new courthouse—wouldn't agree but we only needed a majority. The other two said "Look, you uncovered this Caldwell thing and nobody else would touch it and you ran with it and ran with it and ran with it to the point where there was a lot of serious discussion about whether you were going to get blown up. And you had the courage to do it and nobody else would do it." So they gave us the contract back.

We were also running a free distribution paper in the suburbs that we'd started after we'd realized that the regular paper would never make any money. It did very well in the beginning. We got up to 13,000 circulation. We decided to turn the typesetting shop into a real shop and we began doing newspapers for high schools and nonprofit organizations and we did a lot of government contract work.

My income peaked at about $9,000. As I remember it I was getting paid just enough by the paper to pay the lady who kept the children. In fact several times I just endorsed the check over. But then the paper stopped paying me at one point so for awhile we were living off credit cards. It was just that period when credit cards became a national thing. About every sixty days Marjorie would open the mail and there would be a new credit card from some bank or whatever. They'd say something like, "Because you're a member of the Georgia Bar Association and an excellent credit risk you now have $7,000 of credit."

We would have survived had the daily paper not been so aggressively determined to be a monopoly. When we started the free distribution paper in a particular neighborhood they started one that went to every house in the county. When we agreed to do preprinted inserts at a rate 30 percent below what they were charging they then cut the rate 30 percent below what we were charging in the area where we were doing business. They couldn't make any money publishing the legal ads, because the ceiling was set by the legislature on what you could charge and they had to run the ads in every copy of the paper. But they knew it was our principal source of cash. After we got the contract for the second time they lobbied and lobbied the officials and ran their pictures on the front page and did flattering stories about them. And when that didn't work they helped get two people elected who were willing to change the contract.

That was when we decided to close the paper. We had made a lot of mistakes—journalistic mistakes and commercial mistakes—but this country is not so poor, and Savannah is not so poor, that there wasn't room for someone to make mistakes and still be able to be viable. But when the tenth largest commercial enterprise in town is the daily newspaper and when they are taking 65 percent of all the advertising dollars and every other form of enterprise is splitting the other 35 percent, it strangles any kind of creative impulse. When you tie that together with editorial power there's just no way for anything to get started.

We were killed off by the same forces that are operating throughout the American newspaper industry. That industry's own maturing has managed to close out the source of energy and stimulus for change and competition. It's the same kind of disease that afflicted the auto industry before Toyota and Nissan and Volkswagen taught us how to manufacture cars again. And there is nobody to teach us how to publish newspapers again.

We had about $300,000 in debts, not counting the $200,000 in stock.

We sold the suburban paper and we sold some typesetting equipment and a few other things, all for about $40,000. Another $60,000 was paid off by other members of the enterprise who had cosigned notes or guaranteed various kinds of debt. That left about $200,000. And that's the legacy. We have that instead of a house. We've been paying off our monthly notes and I figure by the time the children get out of high school we'll be able to start making similar payments for college.

Would I do it again? It depends where. But the answer's yes, in about twenty seconds. I don't think Marjorie feels the same way, though. I think she feels it's something you outgrow. I would love to do it again. You cannot enjoy telling stories and not break out in a big smile at the thought of being able to do that. But it would have to be for a purpose. Our paper had that and I consider it to have been a great success. For seven years it changed the way life existed for 200,000 people.

EDNA BUCHANAN:
THE STORY BEHIND THE STORY

It's hard to say why I became a police reporter. I know that as a little kid when I first got hooked on newspapers I was sort of drawn to stories about Willie Sutton and the Mad Bomber and people like that. You do learn more about people on the police beat than any other. And maybe I can identify better with working people, identify better with victims. I know that nothing infuriates me more than when some poor soul gets killed, you know, some Seven–Eleven clerk or somebody on the job somewhere and all he's trying to do is support his family, make a living, do the right thing. I probably had no opinion on the death penalty one way or the other before I got into police reporting but now, as far as I'm concerned, the only thing wrong with it is that they don't carry it out promptly. I probably don't sound like most reporters—most reporters are pretty liberal. Maybe it's the difference in our backgrounds or something.

I really like police reporting but a lot of reporters don't want to do it —they don't want to dirty their hands. And a lot of editors have a built-in prejudice against police stories for some reason; maybe because a lot of them seem to come out of political reporting and so their main interest is in dumb political stories. I discovered that the only key to survival was to outlive them.

The way I operate is mostly just a lot of hard work, a lot of legwork. Usually I start every day by going to the Miami Beach police department, mainly because it's close. And then I go to the Miami police station and then over to Metro, which has seven or eight substations around the county, and I'll just rap with people. The rest I try to get by phone. I talk to cops a lot. There are some who are my friends but I've never gone out drinking in bars with them or anything like that. Talking to cops is the only way to get a lot of the stories I do. Of course a lot of policemen don't recognize a good story so you just have to keep talking to them so it'll come up in conversation.

We also have somebody at the office monitoring the police radios. I used to have a police scanner on my desk but the editors didn't like the noise. I'm always worried now that we'll miss something. One day I walked into the back room where the radios are, to check something out with the guy who was supposed to be listening, and he had all the radios turned down. He was typing a letter applying for another job and he didn't want to be distracted! And these people go to dinner. I've never gone out to dinner or lunch in seventeen years at the *Herald* because that's when things happen. If you walk away for a minute that's when a cop could get shot, or a plane could go down. That's when something could happen that the police want to hush up so they don't do any more transmissions about it. So you have to be listening all the time.

One thing that makes life harder for a police reporter today than it used to be is that all the police reports are on computers. I used to love going into the police stations and reading through the reports, because they were handwritten by the cops or the detectives involved and they could put their own little sense of color in or their own perceptions and you could gather so much about a situation, feeling how the cop felt about it. But now, on these computerized reports, there's no place for anything like that. There's just certain questions to answer, certain places to fill in the blanks. They're like toilet paper, these vast printouts; the human quality isn't there. So what it really means is that we have to go back two steps, to hands-on, person-to-person human contacts.

Like there was a thing on the computer about a robbery where a guy got robbed and knocked down, no big deal. But then I found out that the guy wore artificial legs and he was pushed off his artificial legs for something like a dollar and forty cents. That kind of detail is not going to be in the computer.

I remember one of the last reports that was written before they went to computers was about a robbery victim, Mrs. Margaret McClure. She was an elderly blind woman who lived alone with her two cats, Tippy and Beauty. And she was walking Tippy and Beauty and she got knocked down and mugged and robbed of her last nickel. I wrote the story and of course the good people responded, they always do, and brought her all these wonderful things and somebody paid for her dinner at this little restaurant down the street every night indefinitely. But the only way I knew about her was because a cop wrote in there, on the report, "She was blind and she was walking her cats Tippy and Beauty when she was assaulted from behind." In the computer report they wouldn't say she was out walking her cats. They wouldn't say she's blind.

Even now, though, you can still pick things up from these computer printouts if you're really watching. I used to be the only one going through the police reports but now the *Herald* has these twice-a-week neighborhood tabloids and one time I was in one of the stations and I could tell that the tabloid reporters had been through the reports already but still I saw a little nugget they'd missed. It was a routine missing persons report. There are dozens of missing persons reports in a day but what made this one different were the dates of birth on the person reporting the missing person and the missing person. I said, "Either this has to be a typo or the woman reporting her son missing is a hundred and two years old and the missing son is 74." So I checked into it and sure enough, she was a hundred and two and her son had run away from home. They'd lived together all their lives—he'd been hit by a car and he was sort of a little dotty. He wanted his mother to buy him a car and she wouldn't buy it and so he ran away.

I always like to go out myself to the scene of a crime to see it myself, because you can always write a better story if you've been there. I also always like to talk to the families. I remember a while back I was out of town and came back and went through the cases that had occurred while I was away and there was this one involving a young black guy who had gotten murdered and it was unsolved. I was in the neighborhood one day and I stopped by and knocked on the door of the house where he lived with his grandmother. And she came to answer it and I said, "I'm Edna Buchanan from the *Miami Herald* and I want to talk to you about your grandson's death." And she stepped back and threw open the door and said, "I wondered why you never came," and invited me in. And I thought, "Gee, no one other than the cops had ever come to see her." And I just thought, "My God, I almost drove by; I almost didn't stop." And I was so glad that I did. Because it's important not only to get a better insight into who the people are and who the victims are, and to find out what happened and a lot of the nuances, and to find out if the authorities are really telling the truth, but it also validates the fact that something terrible did indeed happen to them.

I never want to be the one to tell the family, though, that someone has died. But there was one time I did. The Las Vegas police had called me looking for help. They had this body, and cops always want to get the body back to a family; otherwise the taxpayers have to handle it. The guy's name was Teddy and he was a cab driver and he died in this bizarre case that's never been solved. He was found out in the desert next to his cab and he was burned to a crisp. They had to identify him by dental charts. All the police knew was that he'd been out there for seven or eight years and that he'd once driven a cab in Miami Beach. So they checked with the police down here and they had nothing and for some reason they called the newspaper and got to me.

I found out the name of the cab company he'd worked for before—he'd given it as a reference—and I called them and it was easy: they said he'd worked there and that he had a wife named Mary. They didn't know what had happened to her but I did find out he had originally come from Brooklyn, and I thought, "Well, if they split up she might have gone back to Brooklyn." So I called up Brooklyn information and she had a listing, so I got her on the phone. I asked her, "Are you the Mary that was married to Teddy?" and she said "Yeah." And I said to myself, "Shoot, she doesn't know he's dead." So I said, "Well, sit down, are you alright? Teddy is. . .is dead. He died out in Las Vegas."

And there was this big silence. And I thought, "Oh, no, she's probably had a heart attack or something." And then her first words were, "Did he have insurance?"

What had happened was that Teddy had abandoned her and their kid and taken off. And she'd gone back to Brooklyn and raised the kid all by herself. She called me back a couple times to find out anything more she could about any insurance because she wasn't having much luck out in Las Vegas—when they found out they couldn't palm the body off on her they didn't want anything to do with her.

A lot of my stories come from things like that, a telephone call, talking to people. But sometimes they come from tips. That's how I found out about Arthur McDuffie, the black man who was attacked by the police and later died. I heard about it on December 21st, which was a Friday. McDuffie had been attacked on the previous Monday and was in a fatal coma all week. On Friday in the afternoon I got the first call, from someone who said the cops had beat up this black guy on a motorcycle and he was either dead or dying. The person said the cops were claiming they chased him and he crashed but that really they did it and there had been no crash.

So I called the morgue and I said, "Hey, do you have a black guy in there who was killed in a crash while being chased by the police?" And they said no. And I said to myself, "See, just one of these phony tips." And the woman at the morgue said, "But he's on his way, he just died about a half hour ago." And I though, "Oh, no." And that was when I started working on it. And I worked all that night and Saturday and Sunday and the first story ran Monday, Christmas Eve.

One of the first things I did was to call Internal Affairs because when anybody is hurt during an arrest, internal affairs automatically has to investigate it. So I asked if they were investigating the case of McDuffie and they said yes. They had the captain call me back. And he said the investigation was closed. They'd found that nothing untoward had happened: they'd chased him; he was a jerk and he ran and he crashed his motorcycle.

Because the investigation was over I was able to get a copy of the accident report and that was when I first saw the names of some of the guys involved. And I'd seen those names before when we had done this big series about police brutality. They were among the people who had been accused of police brutality and who had been sued the most by citizens, so that made me a heck of a lot more interested in the case.

I also found out from the accident report where they'd taken the motorcycle and I went and looked at it. And that was when I knew that the police had lied, because they'd said they had investigated it. When I walked into the towing garage and said, "Where's Arthur McDuffie's motorcycle?" the guy said, "Oh, I've been wondering when someone was going to come get it. Sign here." And he handed me this clipboard. I could have signed and taken that motorcycle away. And I said, "No, No, I didn't come to claim it; I just want to look at it." And he said, "Well, help yourself, it's over there." If the police really had been investigating the case they wouldn't have let people come in there and paw all over that motorcycle. It would have been confiscated as evidence. As it was, the day the first story appeared they went and confiscated it and then we weren't even allowed to take a picture of it, because it was a major piece of evidence.

The doctor at the morgue had told me that McDuffie's injuries were consistent with those of a motorcycle rider who was hurled over the handlebars and smashed his head on a solid object like a concrete pole or a bridge abutment or a telephone pole. So I went out there to where it happened. But there was no wall, no pole, nothing. It was just an expressway ramp. So I began to wonder, well, maybe he could have hit his head on a curb or something. Because really, in my heart, I didn't want to believe it could have happened the way it did.

I also went out to see the McDuffies. And I really liked them. Eula Mae, the mother, was so heartbroken. She'd gone out to the scene and she showed me that she'd found part of a sharpshooter badge and her son's broken glasses and a strap that I think came from the motorcycle helmet. They showed me all his plaques. He had plaques and plaques and plaques —a whole wall full of plaques. He'd headed a team for this insurance company and his team had consistently won the award every month for selling the most insurance. He also worked with this whole group of kids; he'd taught them how to paint and they had painted a funeral home, the one where he was buried, and he was helping these ghetto kids get jobs and teaching them a trade.

The police later criticized me and criticized the *Herald* because we kept calling him an insurance executive. They thought he was a piece of shit—they wanted him just to be some bad guy that they had to chase. Apparently he did have a traffic record and he had been accused of passing a worthless check once that was never prosecuted. He'd lost his license once and I guess that's why he didn't stop when the police told him to, which was a terrible mistake. Cops get very upset during a chase; they're not only risking their lives, they're risking equipment and they get in trouble if they damage it. So by the time they got to him they were just furious. Blacks will tell you that race was a factor but I don't think so. It is true that the police officer who struck the first blow got in trouble later for kicking black people. But I think Arthur McDuffie, no matter what color he was, probably would have taken a beating that night. Once the first guy hit him, it was like a wild dogpack.

The day the first story came out, a city officer read the morning paper and told his supervisor that he had seen what happened, and that became part of the investigation that was launched, though of course we didn't find that out until later. And we also found out later that two of the cops who had been involved were waiting for the paper to come out that morning, and they raced off to read it alone to figure out how bad things were and whether they could keep on getting away with it. The first story wasn't all that exciting because I had an awful editor but just its appearance made things begin to happen.

I continued to cover the story up to the point of the police officers' arrest. From then on the people who cover the courts took over. I never went to journalism school and I don't know what the official code of ethics is supposed to be but I've always had my own sense of values and I was a little disturbed by some of the stories that began appearing. Because once it got into the court system it was a *big story* and the whole journalism pack was after it, so when they would get a deposition and some police officer who was involved would testify how they jumped up and down on McDuffie's legs to break them and things like that, they would all report every detail. So obviously, you knew there could never be a trial in Miami. And in fact they sent the case off to Tampa, off to redneck country with an all-white jury and they came back pretty quickly with an acquittal.

Of course the verdict came back at the worst possible time on a hot Saturday afternoon. And what followed was a nightmare—seeing that black smoke over the city, seeing the city burning. As I have looked back there is nothing else I could have done. And I know I did the right thing. But what happened because of it afterward was terrible.

I know the paper entered my coverage that year for the Pulitzer, and I thought that if ever I was going to win it would be for that. But I didn't. So after that I didn't think much about the whole thing. When I did win, in 1986, I was actually on vacation—I had taken all my vacation time to work on a book and I didn't even know when the prizes were being announced. Just by coincidence, I think, I was asked to come into the paper for a meeting that day and when I got there I went upstairs and got my mail. I noticed that the newsroom seemed kind of crowded for that time of day and a lot of people were crowded around their terminals. I was about to go to the meeting when this woman I was with said, "Wait, the publisher is going to make an announcement." I didn't know if it was going to be something about the stock going up or the stock going down or what and I just wanted to get the meeting over and go home.

Then it occurred to me that something was strange because the food editor, who I never really got along with, turned around and gave me this funny grin. And then suddenly this big cheer went up from the people around the terminals and the editor sort of jumped up on this desk and announced that I had won a Pulitzer Prize. And I just could not believe it. If I'd had any idea I would have been more ready for it: I would have put on mascara.

The thing that moved me the most about winning the prize was the look I saw in the other reporters' eyes when it was announced. I'm not considered that sociable because I'm always very uptight and focused on work and I don't go to a lot of *Herald* parties or anything. But what I saw in their eyes was that they were really happy for me. And I think my winning showed that somebody out there on the beat, out there in the trenches, not just somebody with some specialty who writes a story or two a year, can win the highest award in journalism. It belonged to all of us; it really did.

20

ALFONSO CHARDY

The Administration and the Contras

IRAN-CONTRA, AS IT BECAME KNOWN, WAS THE CLOSEST thing to a Watergate of the 1980s. Before the scandal was over, the American public found out not only that the Reagan administration had been secretly supplying aid to the Nicaraguan contras, in violation of Congressional prohibitions, but also that officials within the Reagan administration had been involved in selling arms to Iran and diverting profits to contra aid. At the time, Iran was officially regarded as a terrorist state with close links to Lebanese groups responsible for the kidnapping of Americans.

Alfonso Chardy was one of a team of reporters responsible for the *Miami Herald's* winning a Pulitzer Prize in 1987 for the paper's exposure of details of the first aspect of the Iran-contra affair: the contra connection. Chardy is credited with a string of revelations that put the *Herald* out in front on the contra story virtually from the start. Among other things, he established a clear connection between Oliver North, then a member of the National Security Council, and the purportedly "private" contra-supply network. He also supplied details about the links between one of the major figures in the supply network and then-Vice President George Bush.

Chardy says he doubts that the *Herald's* work would ever have become nationally recognized—and Iran-contra a national scandal—if it hadn't been for the fact that television finally became interested in covering the story. "Americans don't read very much," says Chardy, a Mexican national born in 1952, whose guarded manner contrasts with the sharp edge to his observations. "In Mexico or in any Latin American country the people who read, read a lot. And they read the newspapers. In the U.S. I find it more difficult to discuss daily events with Americans at large than I do with citizens of Latin America or Europe."

Chardy believes that television and the entertainment media, not newspapers, are the major agenda-setters in this country. "Everybody knows now about Oliver North and about his secretary, Fawn Hall, but not from reading my stories," he says. "They know that Fawn Hall is dating George Michaels the rock star because it comes out in places like *Rolling Stone* or it's exposed in *Entertainment Tonight*." And, he suggests facetiously, the way to get more Americans interested in what is going on in the world might be to allow them some direct, entertainment-based participation. "If Americans could vote every day by television on whether to give aid to Nicaragua or to El Salvador I think they'd love it," he says. "It would be like *Wheel of Fortune* on a planetary scale."

Following is an excerpt of one of Chardy's stories that formed part of the *Herald*'s award-winning coverage.

THE MIAMI HERALD
October 12, 1986

BUSH, NSC SET UP AID TO REBELS, OFFICIALS SAY
by
ALFONSO CHARDY

WASHINGTON—The National Security Council and the office of Vice President George Bush shared responsibilities in setting up the elaborate anti-Sandinista supply system that came to light with the downing of an American-manned aircraft in Nicaragua last week, knowledgeable administration officials said Saturday.

The administration officials said that while the NSC recruited technical and logistical personnel retired from CIA or Army Special Forces in establishing the network, the vice president's staff concentrated on organizing Cuban exiles in Miami, many of whom were veterans of the CIA-organized Bay of Pigs invasion in 1961. . . .

The role of the NSC and Lt. Col. Oliver North, the NSC's director of political development and political-military affairs, has been widely publicized in the past year.

But the contra connection to Vice President Bush, a former CIA director, had not been generally known, although it was first mentioned publicly in a little-noticed trial in Miami a year ago.

The October 1985 trial involved a private contra supporter, Jesus Garcia, who was charged with illegal possession of a weapon.

Garcia, questioned by Miami Assistant U.S. Attorney Jeffrey Feldman, said that an apparently bogus mission mentioned to him to blow up the Soviet and Cuban embassies in Managua was known as "George Bush's baby."

Garcia, in a telephone interview last summer, said a man identified as Alan Saum, who was the police informant against

Garcia on the weapons charge, also had mentioned Bush's office as his contact point. . . .

The contra link to Bush's office came to light when the only surviving crewman of the downed plane, Eugene Hasenfus, told reporters in Managua Thursday that a Cuban-American veteran of the Bay of Pigs named Max Gomez helped coordinate the intricate aerial supply system serving the contras from El Salvador. . . .

Bush, questioned during a campaign swing through South Carolina Saturday, described Gomez as "a patriot" whom he has met three times. But Bush did not comment on reports that Gomez reported to him on his effort to supply the contras.

ALFONSO CHARDY:
THE STORY BEHIND THE STORY

What really got me interested in journalism were two events in Mexico City in 1968: one was the massive student uprising and the other was the 1968 Olympics. Both of them attracted a large number of foreign reporters. I was a student then and I would approach the reporters and ask them what they did and where they were from, and I was fascinated by their tales about going to the Caribbean or around the world covering things. After I finished preparatory school, which is between high school and college in Mexico, I was in the Army for six months and then I got a job as a galley-proofreader and later a translator at the *Mexico City News*. I had visited the United States but most of my knowledge of English came from taking courses in high school and also by reading and listening to the radio.

From the *News* I went to the Associated Press, which sent me to Buenos Aires and Bogota, and then I became a free-lancer in Central America for the *Miami Herald* and several other publications. In 1980 the *Herald* offered me a job because they needed Spanish-speaking reporters to cover the Mariel boatlift from Cuba to the United States. In 1982 they sent me to Washington to cover U.S. policy toward Latin America.

At the time I began covering the contra affair in Washington I already knew quite a lot about Nicaragua because I had covered the Sandinista revolution in 1978 and 1979, mostly working for UPI. One of the people I had met during that time was Adolfo Calero, who was the manager of the Coca-Cola plant in Nicaragua. Later, he became one of the major contra leaders. I left Nicaragua about two weeks before Somoza was overthrown, after an ABC newsman was killed, and I returned the day after the Sandinistas took over. Everybody in Managua seemed to be elated at that time. A lot of people were coming out of their houses to welcome the Sandinistas as if they were liberators. Everyone was shooting guns up in the air to celebrate. The first statement of the junta people was,

"Stop shooting up in the air because the bullets come back down." I think several people were hurt but I don't think anybody was killed.

I was impressed by the fact that the Sandinistas all seemed to be very, very analytical, which made them different from other Latin American leaders who are generally very rhetorical. They had a plan to socialize Nicaragua, to turn it into a country of idealistic revolution, pretty much like Castro or Ho Chi Minh did. I think they would have been able to implement it had they not run into not just the Reagan administration but, I think, a changed way of thinking around the world, generated by *glasnost* and *perestroika*, that says economic prosperity is more important to the future than resting on your ideological laurels. As it was, they succeeded in withstanding the contra pressures and that is a major triumph. But they have to change and I think they are changing.

I began to encounter Nicaraguans again in the early '80s when I started working for the *Miami Herald* in Florida, because it was during that period that Nicaraguan refugees began to arrive, mostly people from the upper class. I also came into contact with some of the early contra activities; they had some paramilitary training in Florida.

It became well known to those of us in Washington who were covering Latin America and Central America that when Congress moved to end aid to the contras—first they limited U.S. action on behalf of the contras, the so-called Boland amendment, and then they imposed a ban in October of 1984--the administration geared up to find an alternative. All these conservative private benefactors cropped up and I wrote a number of private aid stories. So the next logical step was: Who is promoting all the private aid? Who is supporting them? In conversations with my editor we decided that we were going to go out and see whether the government was really respecting the congressional prohibition.

Within a couple of days I had it confirmed on the record from two contra officials, Calero and Ed Chamorro, that Oliver North was involved. North's name had already cropped up in other publications in connection with the contras but not in connection with private aid. I had already suspected that there was something going on but I had never really posed the question about North's involvement. The contras told me, "Oliver North has come down to Central America to tell us that the Reagan administration will continue helping us no matter what." We spoke in Spanish and I think the language and cultural affinity had something to do with their opening up to me. But I think the main reason was because they didn't realize what all this was going to lead to: how I was going to piece the story together and how that story would become somewhat historic because of the Iran-contra affair. So then I went to a couple of administration officials that I knew were involved in Nicaraguan affairs and I posed the question to them about North's involvement and they confirmed it. My assessment is that they thought as long as it didn't become a major national issue it didn't really matter.

And in fact, after my story came out in June of 1985, it didn't really lead to much. It was the first big story linking Oliver North to circumventing the Boland amendment but basically it was dead in the water. I think somebody on a congressional intelligence committee did put together some questions but that was only after the *New York Times* and the *Washington Post* published their own stories two months later.

From then on the story went in fits and starts. I had to do many other things—cover congressional hearings, attend briefings, and so forth, and every time my editors said, "Well, let's do something on the secret war; let's do something on Ollie North," it was always a struggle to free me up to do some investigating.

So that's how things went along until there was another flurry of stories in 1986 and that's when my editor put together a team of reporters that was the group that won the Pulitzer.

I covered the story the way I cover any other story. The systems may be different in different places but it's all people. The key lies in understanding the process of how gathering information works. The way I do it is that first I plan my piece by figuring out what the theme is going to be. Then I go out like a vacuum cleaner and get as much information as possible about this particular issue, like reading what has already been published and identifying sources, calling them, getting more information, getting the documents. I try to identify the managers of policies, the managers of the issues I'm interested in. Then I read everything that I've got and figure out what the angle is going to be and what I'm going to write.

For me, the real enjoyment of journalism is gathering information and getting it out, so that people read and learn and do whatever they want to do with it—improve democracy or bring about a coup. I just want them to know.

I was always the initiator of the stories about contra aid. Later on, some people called with tips or whatever but even then I still followed the same process. One thing I do is that usually I don't call people on the phone. I jut go over and sit down with them or take them out to lunch or dinner, and I sit down and say, "Hey, I want to talk to *you*." The only source who ever spoke to me because he was troubled by what had been going on was one mid-level administration official who felt the administration's policies were bad for U.S. interests in the region.

Every time I approached a source I would say, "I'd like to quote you by name," but the source—even Congressional aides—always said no automatically. I think in some cases if they were aides they were afraid that if their bosses saw their name in the paper they would be angry at their getting so much publicity. I don't think it's because of the sensitivity of the subject. A lot of them say, "Well, it's a sensitive subject," but I don't think anybody in the U.S. system can agree on what a sensitive subject is —what constitutes national security. I think they all have a general idea but there are no standardized procedures.

There was only one person who lost his job because of me, and that was totally erroneously. This man was an intelligence analyst in the State Department and in one of my stories I quoted "a State Department intelligence official." Memos that came out during the Iran-contra investigations in Congress showed that the analyst was accused of being one of my sources and an investigation of him was begun. But in fact I've never met him. I was quoting another intelligence official.

If we owe the Pulitzer Prize to anyone, it's to the contras. They were the only ones who were willing to be quoted by name. They were the ones who provided the most information, on the record, and sometimes on background, and they continued to do it until the very end and even now. They exposed Oliver North. They exposed Rob Owen. They exposed all the principal people.

I think at the beginning they probably felt that by linking themselves to Oliver North and the administration, even after Congress had prohibited aid, that the Sandinistas, their enemies, would continue to see them as connected to the American government and that would be a signal to the Sandinistas that they still received official backing despite the Congressional prohibition.

Toward the end, I think they were just trying to settle accounts. One faction didn't like Oliver North because he had tried to get rid of that faction. They also wanted to expose Spitz Channell, Oliver North's fundraiser, because they never liked him; they always considered him to be arrogant. So they came to me and said, "Hey, why don't you look into this guy?"

In fact, I think by then they had already concluded that the whole thing was going to unravel. They were far more willing to see the future, far more realistic in their own assessments, than the administration officials, who were saying, "The freedom fighters will go on." I think that after Congress began investigating, the contras wanted to be perceived as not collaborating in a coverup. They realized that Congress was responsible for giving them the money so they wanted to be perceived as forthcoming. Once the Iran-contra affair broke, in conversations with me and other reporters the contras said, "We're going to have to retrench."

I'm sure the contras reported their conversations with me to Oliver North. North knew of my existence and what I was doing but he would never talk to me. I talked to Fawn Hall several times on the phone to ask for an interview and she always turned me down, in a very polite way. There was one memo that came out during the investigation that said that North told Calero to come over and threaten me but Calero always dealt with me in a very friendly way. I think that the reason North talked to other reporters is that they were not asking questions about his *activities,* they were asking questions about his goals.

The administration people understood the process of information, more so than the media do. They read everything and I found them to be very sharp and intelligent and aware. North and his people set up a special "propaganda ministry" that reported to Oliver North and received assistance from the CIA and the Pentagon. There were between fifty and sixty people working there, cultivating network correspondents and trying to influence television and the entertainment industry to support Reagan administration policies in Central America.

I think the first inkling that something really big was going to happen was when the Hasenfus plane was shot down in October of 1986. It came out then that Felix Rodriguez, who Hasenfus said was working for the CIA in the contra supply effort, was one of Bush's acquaintances. I remember that I quickly arranged to meet two sources of mine who knew each other for breakfast on a Saturday morning. They worked in separate agencies but they both worked with Oliver North and one of them knew Bush's people. I asked my sources about Rodriguez and they said, "Oh yeah, people in Bush's office have coordinated this"—the supply effort. I posed the question; they were just responding. I had begun to prepare the story about two days before so then I had the whole thing and I wrote a story for the Sunday paper.

I think the contra issue would still have gone away if it hadn't been for the Iran connection being revealed when a magazine in Lebanon printed a story on it and the networks began picking it up. At first it was just the Iran arms sales. But the minute I saw Oliver North's name raised in connection with the arms sales I said to myself, "This is going to lead to the contras." Within a short time Attorney General Meese gave a news conference and acknowledged that North had diverted profits from the Iran arms sales to the contras. I think they felt that somebody would put two and two together and they figured it would be better if they put it out themselves.

THE
PULITZER PRIZE
BOARD

□

21

ROGER W. WILKINS
A Pulitzer Judge Reflects on a Decade of Change

ROGER WILKINS, FORMER CHAIRMAN OF THE PULTIZER
Prize Board, says that journalism has always had an appeal for him thanks
in large part to memories of his father. The elder Wilkins was a reporter
and later business manager of a black weekly in Kansas City until his death
from tuberculosis when Wilkins was eight. "My father loved words," says
Wilkins, who was born in 1932. "The one present of his that I truly
remember was a dictionary for children; he'd give me a certain number of
words to study each day and we'd discuss them. He was also the only
grown man I have ever encountered who read Shakespeare for pleasure.
With his intellectual drive and his character he could have been one of the
great journalists of his time, but he was prevented by race and illness, and
probably those two were intertwined."

Wilkins' early career included working for a New York law firm,
serving in the Kennedy and Johnson administrations with the eventual
rank of Assistant Attorney General, and working for the Ford Foundation.
In 1972, Wilkins took a job as an editorial writer on the *Washington Post.*
Over the next few months, he wrote a series of carefully constructed
editorials that asked increasingly uncomfortable questions about the role
of Nixon administration officials in the Watergate affair. The editorials,
along with Watergate cartoons by Herblock, were submitted as supple-
mentary material to news articles by Carl Bernstein and Bob Woodward in
the 1973 Pulitzer Prize competition. The *Post* was awarded a Pulitzer Prize
gold medal for public service, a designation that took account of the total
Post effort. In 1974, Wilkins left the *Post* for the *New York Times,* where
for five years he wrote first editorials and later a column combining news
and comment. In 1979, he was elected to the first of three terms on the
Pulitzer Prize Board.

Wilkins, now an author and a professor at George Mason University in Virginia, says that while he enjoyed much of what went with daily journalism, he prefers a more studied approach to issues. "I got so frustrated intellectually with doing enough research to write 968 words, and I'd think, 'Oh, that's pretty interesting,' but then I had to go and write the next 968 words, and the next review, and the next article," he says. "I'm glad I did it but now I want to do something in depth. I want to read ten books about the same thing."

To listen to Wilkins is to hear a man thinking his way through life, mulling over subjects that range from the disintegration of America's inner cities to the reasons why journalism is a particularly difficult field for women or people of color. One of those reasons, he says, is that journalism is so personal. "What you have to offer as a journalist is the sum and substance of what you are: your capacity to see, understand and recreate some human experience," Wilkins says. "Then you hand it in, and if somebody says, 'That flunks,' it isn't just that you couldn't hit the curve ball today; it's that you flunk, as a human being. At most other institutions, you do your work, you have your fights at the office, you get your money, and you go home. But in the newspaper business, much more of your self, much more of your essence, is on the line every day. So if you're a woman or a black or an hispanic you're in constant turmoil because you never know where the line is between your deficiencies and their limitations. You've never quite sure what's them and what's you."

Wilkins says that when he was finishing a year as the first black chairman of the Pulitzer Prize Board, he suggested to his colleagues that they ought to pause and reflect on that moment. "For my own part, it was a time I dedicated to my father and my father's memory," Wilkins says. "I know he would have just exploded with joy to see his son as chair of the Pulitzer Prize Board."

Following are Wilkins' thoughts on that experience.

ROGER WILKINS:
THE PULITZER PRIZE BOARD

My decision to quit the *New York Times* and my joining the Pulitzer Board came at almost the same time. I was cleaning out my desk when I got a call from the president of Columbia University saying that I'd been elected to the Pulitzer Board. At first I thought he was asking me to be on a Pulitzer jury but then I thought, no, the president of Columbia doesn't call you to ask you to be on a jury. I said, "Well, I can't do that because I've quit the *Times*. I'm no longer a daily journalist." He said that it didn't matter, all I had to do was to say yes. So I said yes.

It turned out that the board at that point had decided to come out of the Dark Ages. They had never had a woman or a black on the board. That year they elected Hannah Gray, the first nonjournalist on the board apart from the president of Columbia, and two blacks, Bill Raspberry and me. The first year I was on the board, 1980, I didn't say much. I was really young by comparison with a lot of the members, who were in their mid-60s, because at that time you could serve three four-year terms—it's now three three-year terms. My recollection was that I was not overwhelmed by the depth and the profundity of the debate and conversation. I mean it wasn't stupid, and some of it was quite thoughtful, but there was a good deal of the old-boy harumphing.

The longer I was on the board, the younger and smarter I thought it got. I also felt by the end of my nine years that while the makeup of the board was still not terrific, the fact was that non-standard Americans, as I call people who aren't white males, were better represented and better respected and more powerful in that group than they are in almost any other place of significance and power in America.

My first year on the board was the year that the *Washington Post* won a Pulitzer Prize and then gave it back after finding out that its reporter, Janet Cooke, had made up her story about a young heroin addict.

I think all of us on the board had found the story shocking and powerfully compelling and a piece of extraordinary reporting as well. It never occurred to any of us that there might be doubts in the heads of the editors at the *Post* and I was totally unaware of the whispered controversy within the *Post* newsroom about whether the story was true.

When it came out that it wasn't, the heat was awful. A lot of people are jealous of the people who are on the board, and some desperately want a prize. A lot of the fury against the Pulitzer process was unleashed. And because Janet Cooke was black, I was concerned about what would happen in newsrooms where white editors already looked at you funny if you were black and where a lot of them had this view that black people couldn't think so well.

In my opinion, there's no foolproof way to prevent something like the Janet Cooke incident, but we did decide to institute some reforms that I think are very good. One was to give more time to meet and reflect— two full days in the spring and another day in the fall for business. We also instituted a policy of consulting more with juries before shifting pieces from one category to another.

Over the years, I came to look forward to the discussions that we had on the Pulitzer Board. Each year in February and March I did little else except read Pulitzer entries, and I would go into the meetings with notes on each category I'd read. The journalism prizes were done first, by the committee of the whole. The chairman would say, for example, "Now we're going to do public service," and the hands would go up, just like in school. If you were a good chair, once the conversation began to take shape you regulated it and eventually someone would make a motion or you would ask for a motion on awarding the prize.

I have seen people come into the room and say, "I just believe that this entry is the one that ought to get the gold medal for public service," and then two or three people would agree and you would see a consensus forming. And then somebody would say, "Yes, but just look at the third story in the entry, just look at this lead, it is not well-constructed, look at the art work throughout, and now, just look at this other entry," and you could see the consensus melt. People would bring to bear the full force of their experience and sometimes it really was wonderful to see the kind of accumulated force of this journalistic intellect being applied.

If there is an affirmative action impulse on the board, it is unspoken, because the ethos is to reward the best journalism, not to spread the awards around. I never wanted to give a prize to a minority or a woman just because that person was a minority or a woman, but I always wanted to make sure that my presence had the impact of making sure than every woman and every minority that came before the board got their due. One of the things about being black is that you don't even have to say anything to change the discourse; just because you're there people change. The same is true with being a woman. There were times when a black person got a prize when I just wondered what would have happened in earlier days. Now don't get me wrong; I don't think that these people's work did not merit the prize. I'm simply saying that blacks got the kind of consideration they were due because there were some black people sitting on that board, consideration that they might not otherwise have got.

It could also work the other way. I remember very clearly one year there was a lot of sentiment for a prize for a certain writer. I didn't know this person, but based solely on the submissions, I believed that some of the work this person had done was insensitive on the grounds of race. I made the case, and I could see people change, and think, "Well, gee, I didn't think of that; boy I didn't see it that way." If I hadn't said what I said, this person would have won a prize.

One of the things I hoped as a judge was that the prizes that were given to non-standard Americans would send a message to the editors of this world saying, "Look how terrific these people can be. The talent is spread around. God did not funnel all the journalistic talent into the minds and spirits of white males, so look around, fellows." But I don't really think of the Pulitzer Prize Board or process as a mechanism to change the demographics of journalism.

As for expanding what kinds of journalism are considered or who the judges will be, I think the board is more sensitive to more issues and has a more sophisticated and fluid view of journalism than it did, but you have to remember that it's only in the past nine years that the board has been anything other than publishers and editors, white, male, the most establishment of the establishment figures in journalism. It is a long reach from Clayton Kirkpatrick of the *Chicago Tribune* and Lee Hills of Knight-Ridder to the *Berkeley Barb*. That's a very long trip. You're talking about a board and a process that has just begun to change.

AFTERWORD

SOME MONTHS AFTER I'D INTERVIEWED GENE MILLER OF the *Miami Herald* for this book, he wrote to me with some further thoughts about the Pulitzer Prizes.

"Sure, the prize selection process today is fraught with politics, freak chance, dumb luck, and uneven categories," Miller wrote. "A superb entry will get knocked out one year because of competition and a dog will prevail the next year for lack of it. . . . The point is, though, that the prize establishes, if not demands, a standard of excellence. It is a measure recognizable in newsrooms everywhere. . . .

"I work for Knight-Ridder. John S. Knight, an opinionated man not averse to making a buck, wrote thoughtfully and passionately about the Vietnam War and won a Pulitzer in 1968. I don't remember how much money his newspapers—or anyone else's—made that year. I know, though, that newspaper excellence, as reflected in Pulitzers, was more important than an obsession with ever-increasing earnings-per-share. I'm not sure that is true anymore."

If there is one overriding problem that will be facing journalists in the last quarter-century leading up to the one-hundredth anniversary of the Pulitzer Prizes, I believe it will be the one that Miller touches on: how to balance economic interests and news values. Many of the Pulitzer winners I spoke with made reference to it in one way or another. Hanson Baldwin, who got his start in journalism only a few years after the inception of the Pulitzer prizes, ruefully recalled the demise of the *New York Times'* occasional practice of announcing on the front page that it couldn't print all its scheduled advertising because there was too much news. Albert Scardino mourned the passing of his little Georgia weekly and questioned whether a similar undertaking could ever hope to succeed, given the rapid trend toward large, monopolistic news organizations.

It is a trend that shows no sign of abating. Media critic Ben Bagdikian

noted in an article in 1985 that forty-three giant companies, by his count
—down from fifty just four years before—controlled most of the daily
newspapers, magazines, TV and radio stations, book publishers and movie
studios in the United States. In 1989, Time Inc. and Warner Communications combined forces to produce the world's largest media-entertainment
company. Along with this consolidation came rising Wall Street interest in
the media and a greater awareness of the bottom line.

Some journalists have reacted to the new developments with alarm,
expressing the fear that business considerations will lead to an ever-greater
focus on news as a commodity rather than as a public service. In a 1990
article in the *Washington Journalism Review,* Bill Kovach, former editor
of the *Atlanta Journal* and *Constitution,* was quoted as saying, "It's the
pressure to always grow that changes the nature of journalism. It has more
territory and wants to offend fewer people." Other journalists, however,
like Michael Fancher, executive editor of the *Seattle Times,* are excited by
what they see as new possibilities. In a 1987 article in the *Gannett Center
Journal,* Fancher wrote that, equipped as he was with business training, he
had "the opportunity to change the newspaper in qualitative ways from
within the editor's role." Said Fancher, "Some editors resist getting involved in the *business* of newspapering, fearful they will be tainted by
filthy lucre. I believe those editors are doomed. Sooner or later, their
journalistic options will be proscribed by someone else's bottom line. It's a
fact of modern business life."

My own view is that while there is no question that media companies
have become increasingly like other corporations—most newsrooms look
more like insurance offices than like any set out of *The Front Page*—it is
impossible to generalize about what is happening and what it means long-
term for the quality of news. In 1987, I went to Detroit to write about
what had changed at the *Detroit News,* formerly a family-owned organization, following its purchase by the giant Gannett corporation a year earlier.
What I found was that opinions within the paper about the effect of the
Gannett purchase were all over the lot, while outside, most ordinary
readers didn't notice much difference. Several years before, I'd found the
same thing while writing about Rupert Murdoch's purchase of the London
Times. Of far more potential significance in Detroit was the joint operating
agreement between the *News* and the Knight-Ridder chain's *Free Press*
that went into effect in late 1989. Under the agreement—one of about 20
similar arrangements throughout the country—the papers will maintain
separate news staffs but merge their business operations and share profits.

The danger in such agreements—which amount to monopolies—is that owners can reduce the quality of their newspapers without worrying about the financial effect of losing readers or advertisers.

The few serious studies on the effect of changes in media ownership have tended to end up without definitive conclusions: perhaps because the changes are not there to be found, perhaps because the right questions haven't been asked, or perhaps, as a group of Rand Corporation researchers suggested, because the effects are "qualitative and too subtle" to be measured quantitatively. And of course no study can measure how much of what is happening reflects not changes in the news business but rather changes in the culture of which the news industry is a part. In the 1980s, those changes included a growing fascination with business, particularly on the part of the young, that made notions of public service seem at times quaintly out of date. Many journalists, perhaps sensing the power of forces over which they had no control, seemed to lose heart.

Issues of size and of business versus news values are hardly the only concerns facing news organizations. Credibility has emerged as a subject of great worry among news executives as the public admiration induced by the uncovering of the Watergate scandal has given way to more critical scrutiny. A 1973 Harris poll found that 30 percent of those polled in a nationwide survey said they had "a great deal of confidence" in the press; by 1989, that number had dropped to 18 percent. (It's only fair to note, however, that almost all major institutions suffered substantial drops in confidence; further, while the public's confidence in the press was less than its confidence in the military and the Supreme Court in 1989, the press came out ahead of major companies and organized religion.) Two companion studies in the mid-1980s, both sponsored by press organizations, found that journalists had an enormously higher opinion of their factual accuracy and objectivity than did the public.

Such findings would certainly accord with the opinion of at least one press critic, Alexander Cockburn, who commented in a 1984 column in the *Wall Street Journal* that American journalists seem preoccupied with patting each other on the back but never get around to any serious self-reflection. "Year after year this undignified prize-giving ritual goes on, without any apparent qualms on the part of my profession," the British-born Cockburn wrote. "Why?. . .One answer could be that journalists are, by nature and social function, racked with feelings of insecurity and inferiority; to alleviate those pangs, British journalists turn to drink and American ones to prizes."

COUPLE GUNNED
DOWN—NEWS AT TEN

OTHER FIVE STAR TITLES BY LAURIE MOORE

Constable's Run (2002)
The Lady Godiva Murder (2002)
Constable's Apprehension (2003)
The Wild Orchid Society (2004)
Constable's Wedding (2005)
Jury Rigged (2008)
Woman Strangled—News at Ten (2009)
Deb on Arrival—Live at Five (2010)

COUPLE GUNNED DOWN—NEWS AT TEN

LAURIE MOORE

FIVE STAR

A part of Gale, Cengage Learning

GALE
CENGAGE Learning™

Detroit • New York • San Francisco • New Haven, Conn • Waterville, Maine • London

GALE
CENGAGE Learning

LIBRARY OF CONGRESS CATALOGING-IN-PUBLICATION DATA

Moore, Laurie.
    Couple gunned down, news at ten / Laurie Moore. — 1st ed.
        p. cm.
    ISBN-13: 978-1-4328-2528-7 (hardcover)
    ISBN-10: 1-4328-2528-3 (hardcover)
    1. Women television journalists—Fiction. 2. Texas—Fiction. I.
Title.
    PS3613.O564C69 2011
    813'.6—dc22   2011007421

First Edition. First Printing: June 2011.
Published in 2011 in conjunction with Tekno Books.

Printed in the United States of America
1 2 3 4 5 6 7 15 14 13 12 11